W9-BJK-640

# SUPER SOCCER

## Skills & Drills
## For Players & Coaches

NASL All-Star Ray Hudson
with Dan Herbst

**THE BODY
PRESS**

## ABOUT THE AUTHORS

Ray Hudson (left) and Dan Herbst (right) are soccer experts. Ever since he arrived in the United States in 1977, Ray Hudson has been a star of the professional soccer scene. He's a four-time North American Soccer League (NASL) all-star. He played in 197 regular season matches, scoring 44 goals from his midfield position while achieving 99 assists. He's ranked third in league history in that category behind only Vladislav Bogicevic and Karl-Heinz Granitza. Ray is now with the Minnesota Strikers of the Major Indoor Soccer League (MISL).

In addition, Ray is a great communicator. For several seasons he wrote a column for the *Fort Lauderdale News* and *Sun-Sentinel*.

Dan Herbst is a former high-school and college soccer star who now coaches high-school soccer in New York state. He's toured Great Britain as both player and coach. However, he's best known as a soccer journalist, writing for many soccer publications.

**This book is dedicated to the loving memory of
Zelda Herbst (1918-1985).**

**Published by The Body Press, a division of HPBooks, Inc.**
P.O. Box 5367, Tucson, AZ 85703    602/888-2150
ISBN: 0-89586-358-8    Library of Congress Catalog No. 85-73183
©1986 HPBooks, Inc.    Printed in U.S.A.
1st Printing

# CONTENTS

Foreword ................................. 4

Introduction ............................. 5

1 Soccer Basics ......................... 10

2 Trapping & Ball Control .............. 24

3 Heading ............................... 38

4 Dribbling ............................. 48

5 Passing ............................... 65

6 Shooting & Scoring ................... 86

7 Defending ............................ 104

8 Goalkeeping ......................... 119

9 The Mental Game .................... 141

USSF Soccer Laws ................. 154

**Publisher**
Rick Bailey

**Editorial Director**
Theodore DiSante

**Editorial Consultants**
Michael Taylor
Harry McLaughlin

**Art Director**
Don Burton

**Book Design**
Kathleen Koopman

**Typography**
Cindy Coatsworth
Michelle Carter

**Director of Manufacturing**
Anthony B. Narducci

**Illustrations**
Allan Mogel

**Front Cover Photo**
George Tiedemann

**Back Cover Photo**
Steve A. Merzer

Material prepared by
Rutledge Books, a division of
Sammis Publishing
Corporation, 122 E. 25th St.,
New York, NY 10010

# Foreword

When I was growing up on Long Island in the late 1960s, soccer was a lot different from what it is today. At that time, some high-school soccer players were guys who weren't good enough athletes to participate on their football teams. Others played primarily to keep in shape for other sports. For me, soccer was a great way to stay in condition for "serious" games like basketball and tennis. Things sure have changed!

Today, soccer's popularity easily eclipses many other "traditional" North American sports. Literally millions of kids are kicking balls from Miami to Vancouver and everywhere in between. Domestic youth-club teams are now competing on equal footing with their South American and European counterparts. And scores of American-born athletes are holding our own in the professional ranks.

This great boom has been reflected on school campuses too. Crowds, quality of play, stadium facilities and scholarship availability have all advanced greatly. Soccer is here to stay, undeniably the most popular sport among America's youth.

It isn't hard to understand why. This is a fun game in which all players get to run, kick, attack and defend. It's great exercise, relatively injury-free and very economical.

Unlike many other team sports, size is not a prerequisite for success. In fact, Péle, widely recognized as the greatest player of all time, stands 5 feet 8 inches.

However, with this boom has come some growing pains. Good soccer fields are difficult to find. Because few adults played this game in their childhoods, there's a shortage of qualified coaches and referees.

Chances are, you are either one of millions of players or one of hundreds of thousands of parents who've become involved because of your children. If you are a parent, you may well be a volunteer coach or referee.

Ray and Dan tell you everything you need to know about maximizing your soccer skills — as parent or player. But they also stress the most important part of the game — *having fun*.

Alan Mayer
1982-83 Major Indoor Soccer
League's Most Valuable Player

# Introduction

Soccer is one of the easiest games to learn. But it's also one of the toughest games to master. Rules are simple to understand. And the game's structure gives players freedom to move that is unavailable in most other sports.

Known in England as *Association Football,* or just *Football,* soccer is a game played all over the world. You can be certain that no matter what time of day you're reading this, thousands of people are kicking soccer balls somewhere on this planet. Because of its universal appeal, soccer never sleeps.

Nor, for that matter, can a player "nap" during a game. Soccer's action is constant, demanding skill, intelligence and fitness of its participants. Unlike most American team sports, it is a game in which all positions are of nearly equal importance. In soccer, every player is the "quarterback" or "pitcher" when he has the ball. *All* athletes must perform well for the team to succeed.

On the following pages, I introduce the basics of the game from step one—how soccer is played—through the various methods of ball control. I highlight each skill with an explanation of what to do, in addition to common pitfalls to avoid. And I offer many helpful drills and games you can play on your own or with friends to improve your techniques.

## YOU NEED DEDICATION

I'm often asked what is the most important attribute for a young player. In my opinion, the key ingredients are a love of the game and a desire to improve. I'm encouraged that you're taking the time and effort to read this book. This demonstrates that you want to achieve something positive the next time you play. It also means that you enjoy soccer. That's something we have in common.

From as far back as I can remember, soccer has been as much a part of my daily life as eating and sleeping. My father, Wilf, was a good amateur player in his day. He loves the sport with all his heart, just like I do. In fact, even on my wedding day he was quite upset because one of his favorite players had been left out of the lineup for a key World Cup match!

## IT'S INTERNATIONAL

A passion such as my Dad has for the game is as universal as soccer itself. Soccer matches and personalities have been associated with both wars and truces alike. More than one head of state is said to have retained his position because his nation won the World Cup, soccer's greatest prize. No president, pope or king is as recognizable in as many places as Péle, soccer's all-time greatest star.

The unparalleled internationalism of this sport is one of its greatest attributes. Even if you think you have nothing in common with people in Asia, Africa, the Mideast, South America, Europe or anywhere else, you probably share the game of soccer.

To me, that's very important. When my team, the Ft. Lauderdale Strikers, advanced to Soccer Bowl-80, our roster included players from countries as different as Peru, West Germany, Chile, Holland, Canada, South Africa, Brazil, England and, of course, the United States. Working with men of such divergent backgrounds for several seasons taught me how much we had in common. It's very hard to be narrow-minded or prejudiced when you get to know people from other cultures well.

Best of all, you don't have to be a professional or collegiate star to share that experience. Literally hundreds of youth tournaments are held worldwide with participants from several countries. Now that soccer is popular in North America, many of our teams are traveling abroad, as well as playing host to foreign clubs.

I've heard countless stories from Striker fans of youngsters who've made great friends in distant lands through soccer.

Left: Soccer, even at the professional level, is all about having fun. (Jann Zlotkin)

I love teaching young athletes. They've been known to teach me a thing or two along the way! (Jim Frank)

## THE BASIC APPEAL

Of course, the bottom line behind soccer's popularity is basic. It's simply a great game for both boys and girls to play. Soccer is safe, exciting, fast and inexpensive. There are leagues for kids, senior citizens and those of us in between.

As you can tell, I really do love this sport. I'm thrilled at how it's grown in North America over the past few years. I've seen incredible improvements in the quantity and quality of North American soccer in the past few years. In fact, there are many North American soccer pros who could more than hold their own in any league in the world.

Of course, all has not been roses. Anything that grows so rapidly is bound to experience growing pains. Soccer is no exception. With the boom in participation, particularly at the youth level, has come a commensurate demand for coaches and referees. But because very few adults played soccer as youths, there isn't a very large pool of experienced people to draw from for these important positions.

If you're one of those who volunteered when your son or daughter signed up to play soccer, this book will help. I present you with a solid foundation of easy-to-understand information that will guide you through the months ahead.

Moreover, the most important goals of a youth coach are to make the experience both worthwhile and enjoyable for your players. I'll offer pointers on how to do both later in the book.

A message to you female readers: Throughout this book you'll see *he* and *him* used a lot. This doesn't imply that only boys and men play soccer or will benefit from this book. This is merely general usage because the English language doesn't have a pronoun (yet!) that stands for both males and females.

# CHAPTER ONE

# Soccer Basics

Let's start at the beginning by looking at the *laws* of soccer, the roles of its various positions and some basic terminology. In this chapter, the laws are discussed generally. Current United States Soccer Federation (USSF) laws start on page 154.

## LAWS OF THE GAME

In soccer, we refer to regulations as the *laws* of the game. *Rules,* in soccer parlance, are merely the flexible standards that can change from league to league, such as the duration of matches.

**No Hands**—The law that makes soccer unique among team sports commonly played in North America is that *all but one* of the 11 players on a team are prohibited from intentionally using hands or arms to control or redirect the ball in the field of play. Only the *goalkeeper* is exempt—and only within a limited area.

A soccer player must be able to master a sphere a bit smaller than a basketball by using feet, thighs, chest and, yes, even head. The basic challenge is to get the ball into your opponent's goal as many times as possible during a match.

Your instinct to catch or throw the ball must be subdued in favor of other skills requiring tremendous coordination and practice. When they are mastered, there is little in sport as impressive as watching an athlete control a ball with his body as apparently effortlessly as if he had used his hands.

A hand ball, such as this, results in a direct free kick for the other team. (Jim Frank)

**Goalkeeper**—Also called the *goalie,* the goalkeeper tries to keep the ball from entering his team's 24x8-foot goal. To do that, he is allowed to use any part of his body, including hands and arms. But he is restricted to the 44x18-yard penalty area directly in front of the net. Should he leave that zone to play the ball, he is bound by the same limitations as all other players. Outside of the zone, he is prohibited from using his hands.

**Free Kick**—If the goalie violates that law, the other team is awarded a *direct free kick* from the point of the infraction. In this case, the team given possession may shoot the ball straight into the opponents' goal.

Less-serious fouls are penalized by an *indirect free kick*. It's different in that at least two players must touch the ball before a goal is scored. This is soccer justice—a less serious foul is "punished" by an action that is less likely to result in a goal.

Holding is another direct-free-kick foul. (Jim Frank)

Whether the penalty is a direct or indirect offense, all of the fouling team's players must be at least 10 yards from the ball until it is put back into play. The only exception is for an indirect free kick awarded within 10 yards of the fouling side's goal.

As I said, the game's laws are fairly simple. Direct-free-kick fouls, called for intentionally handling the ball, are also called when there is a *serious* form of illegal body contact. You may not kick, push, hold, strike, punch, trip or jump at an opponent. In addition, you may not charge at him violently or from his back. Any one of these is a direct-free-kick offense.

However, not all body contact is prohibited. For instance, a shoulder-to-shoulder charge is OK as long as you are playing the ball.

An indirect free kick is called for less serious violations. For example, if you put yourself between an opponent and the ball to impede his movement toward the ball when the ball isn't within playing distance, you've obstructed the opponent. You have denied him his rightful chance to play the ball. This is officially known as *obstruction*.

Another example of an indirect-free-kick foul would be when you commit a *dangerous play* that jeopardizes either an opponent or yourself. This is illegal even though no contact may have resulted.

Let's say the ball is at head height and a few inches in front of your rival's face. In that situation, it would be OK for you to attempt to redirect the ball with your head. However, if you try to kick the ball, thereby exposing the underside of your cleated shoe to the other player's face, you've put him in danger.

In contrast, if the ball is at knee height and you try to kick it as the opponent attempts to hit it with his head, his unnatural action places *him* in danger. The foul would be his.

A goalie also commits an indirect-free-kick foul when he takes more than four steps while in possession of the ball.

By kicking her foot unnaturally and, in doing so, endangering her opponent, the player at left is called for a *dangerous play*. (Jim Frank)

**Penalty Kick** — If a team is guilty of a direct-free-kick foul within its own penalty area, a *penalty kick* is awarded to the opposing team. A penalty kick almost always results in a score. The ball is placed 12 yards in front of the middle of the 192-square-foot goal area. The goalie must stand with at least a part of each foot on his goal line. He may not move his feet until the ball has been kicked. All players except the goalie and the attacking team's shooter must vacate the penalty area until the ball has been kicked.

**Other Fouls**—Young players and some coaches often share the misconception that the severity of a foul determines whether the resulting kick is deemed direct or indirect. That is not the case! Any trip is a direct-free-kick offense, whether or not it was violent or accidental.

However, if in the referee's opinion a player tries to physically injure an opponent, a further sanction may be instituted. The athlete committing the foul may be issued a *caution*. This means that any more serious misconduct will expel him from the match. Or the player is *ejected*, meaning that his team is prohibited from using a substitute for the punished player. The referee indicates such calls by holding up a yellow or red card, respectively.

In fact, any unsporting action by a player or coach may be so penalized. Common examples include arguing with an official in an impolite manner, spitting at an opponent, committing a foul to gain a tactical advantage, cursing or deliberately wasting time before putting the ball back into play.

**Officials**—Most soccer matches are governed by three officials. I can't say three *men* because there are many outstanding female officials, including a very talented one who has worked as a *lineswoman* in the North American Soccer League.

There are two linesmen and one *referee*. Linesmen assist the referee, whose judgments are final. Only the *ref* has a whistle and can make a call. Linesmen are positioned along the sideline and rarely venture onto the field of play. Linesmen use flags to signal the referee when the ball goes *into touch*, meaning out of bounds, when an attacker is offside, or when they see a foul they think the referee might have missed. Essentially, they serve as extra eyes for the ref, who is in the middle of the action.

The ref tries to stay close enough to the play to see all the action—usually within 15 yards of the ball—without hindering players' movements. If the ball should inadvertently touch the referee, it is still in play. In that respect, the referee is no different from a goalpost or corner flag. He is considered a part of the field!

In some areas and leagues, especially at the scholastic level, games are officiated by two referees of equal stature. While this system is more economical for schools, it is not as effective as the more common one-ref/two-linesmen system universally used in professional soccer.

**Playing Field**—As shown on page 17, a soccer field, or *pitch*, has two goals, one in the middle of each goal line. Penalty areas in front of them signify the territories in which a goalie may use his hands and where any direct-kick foul against the defending team results in a penalty kick.

He may not always be right, but he is the referee. Treat him with respect! (Steve Merzer)

Within the penalty area is another rectangle—a 20x6-yard box directly in front of the goal. Its only significance is that all *goal kicks* must be made from within its boundaries. This occurs when the attacking team last touched the ball before it crossed over the goal line. The defending team makes a goal kick to put the ball back in play.

When the defending side knocks the ball over its own goal line, a *corner kick* restarts play. The ball is placed within a yard of the corner of the field that is closest to where the ball left the playing area—such as the right corner when the ball traveled past the right side of the goal. A member of the attacking team kicks the ball back into play.

The goal kick restarts play when the attacking team last touched the ball before it crossed the goal line. (Almar Photo Ltd.)

Incidentally, should that person boot the ball directly into his team's goal, the score counts. As with all forms of free kicks, all members of the defending side must stay at least 10 yards from the ball until it is kicked.

Similarly, on goal kicks no member of the opposite team is permitted in the penalty area until the ball is put into play. The ball must leave the penalty box before it can be touched by a member of either team. Any violations result in the kick's being made again.

Whenever the ball crosses over the *sideline,* a different method of restart is used. The team not touching the ball last before it left the field is awarded possession. The ball is then *thrown* into play. Specific throw-in regulations are covered later. Just note that this is the only time when a non-goalie may use his hands. And, he must stand outside the field of play when making the throw.

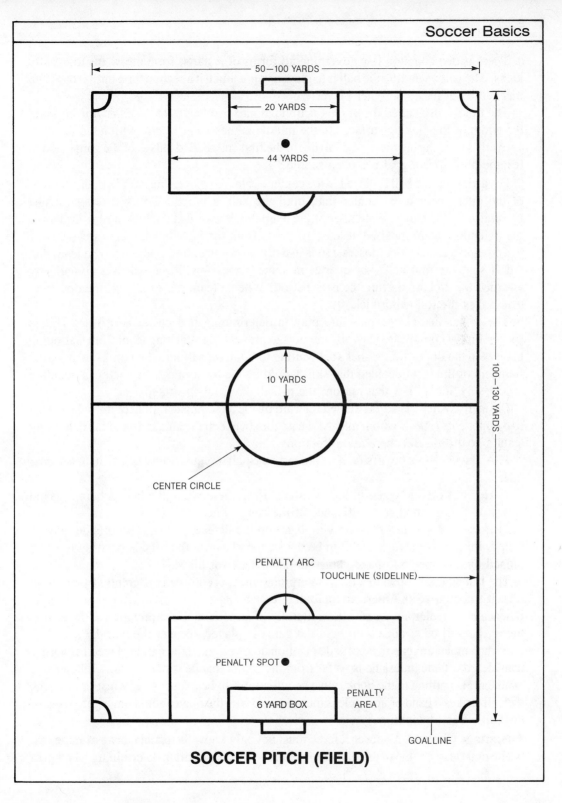

**SOCCER PITCH (FIELD)**

There is one common law governing all forms of restarts, from throw-ins to penalty kicks. The person putting the ball into play may not touch it a second time until it has been touched by at least one other player.

The field—also called the *pitch*—is divided into two halves by a *center line* crossing the width of the playing surface. In the middle is the *center circle,* with a radius of 10 yards. It's used during the *kickoff,* to begin the first and second halves of the game, and to resume play after a goal has been scored.

For a kickoff, the ball is placed in the center circle. All players must be in their own half of the pitch, behind the center line, until the ball is propelled forward at least one revolution of the ball by a member of the team that is awarded the kick. All members of the defending team must be at least 10 yards from the ball, outside the circle.

To begin a match, first possession is usually determined by a coin toss. The team that didn't start the first half—or quarter in some places—with the ball is automatically awarded the kickoff starting the next period. When a team scores a goal, the opposing team takes the following kickoff.

The center line also comes into play in determining if a player is *offside*. This is soccer's most complicated law. Its intent is to prevent the attacking team from stationing players in the opposition's goal area waiting to boot the ball into the net. Long ago, the founders of the sport decided that skill would be the most important factor in deciding soccer superiority. For that reason, the offside law was instituted.

Basically, when the ball is played forward by the attacking team, there must be at least two opponents (one of whom may be the goalie) between the attackers and the defending team's goal line. But there are exceptions:

1) A player cannot be offside if he receives the ball directly from a throw-in or a corner kick.

2) He isn't offside when in his own half of the field while the ball is being played forward. This is another significance of the center line.

3) If the ball was last played by a player on the defending team, no offside may be called. Furthermore, for the call to be made, the player in the offside position must be judged by the referee to have gained an advantage for his side.

The last clause is open to a lot of interpretation. It is enforced differently by different refs. It's not unlike an American football referee being able to call holding on every play if he wanted to interpret the rule book literally. If an official's interpretation of the laws is literal, he will be at odds with how the game is played all over the world.

For example, anyone in an offside position at the moment the ball is played forward is considered offside unless he is so far from the action that he is not a factor. Likewise, a hand ball, according to the book, must be intentional to be a foul. A ref whistles any time the ball strikes a hand or arm unless there was no way the player could have gotten out of the ball's line of flight.

**Advantage Clause**—A soccer referee must not only know the official laws of his sport, but he must also be able to use discretion. This is a decisive part in determining whether or not to use the *advantage clause*. It states that if calling a foul would harm the victimized side, the referee is permitted to let play continue.

To illustrate this, let's consider the following hypothetical example: You have the ball and are advancing toward the other team's goal with a three-man-on-one advantage. The lone defender, knowing he has little chance to thwart the attack legally, intentionally trips one of your players outside the penalty area.

If the referee calls the foul at this point, the resulting direct-free kick would hurt your team. You would have less chance to score than if play had continued. Thus, the defender who intentionally violates a law would be rewarded for his action. Obviously, justice would not be served.

Instead, the referee permits play to continue because it is more advantageous to the team that was fouled. Should he wish, the ref can still caution or eject the guilty party when play stops.

Keep in mind that once the referee decides to allow play to continue, he can not subsequently call the foul should the ball be lost immediately thereafter.

I've talked to plenty of referees and they all insist that this is the toughest decision to make. It is human instinct to call a foul as soon as it occurs. This is how most other sports work. A tip to you novice officials: Try carrying your whistle in your hand, not your mouth. This way you have an extra split-second to evaluate the situation before making the call.

With rare exception, the advantage clause is used only when the ball carrier is in the open and has advanced past the point of the infraction while moving toward the opposition's goal. Rarely is it used when the fouled player is deep in his own half of the field.

**Variations of the Game**—Field dimensions vary, but no field is small. All must be at least 100 yards long and can be as long as 130 yards. Width varies from 50 to 100 yards. Typical dimensions at the collegiate and pro levels are 110x70 yards. In youth soccer, the field may be much smaller.

That's a lot of territory for a referee to cover. Obviously, it's essential for soccer officials to be fit. In fact, North American Soccer League (NASL) referees, and those in most major leagues throughout the world, are required to pass fitness tests to ensure they can stand 90 minutes of demanding work.

Most games consist of two halves of 45 minutes each. But they may be shorter. As a rule, the younger the participants, the shorter the game. The United States Youth Soccer Association (USYSA), the official governing body of U.S. soccer for players under age 19, recommends that athletes under 10 years play two halves of 25 minutes each.

The USYSA recommends increasing the length of play up to the full 90 minutes for senior players. You can get these guidelines from your state association, which is affiliated with the parent body, or directly from the USYSA.

**Team Laws**—Each team consists of 11 players, including the goalkeeper. The goalie must wear a uniform with colors that clearly distinguish him from his teammates, opponents and officials.

Historically, soccer was literally an 11-man game. Not until the 1970 World Cup were substitutions allowed in international competitions. In fact, in the pro game today a team is permitted only two changes per match. An athlete leaving the game in favor of a substitute may not return. Should a team use its two substitutions and subsequently have a man injured, it must continue with 10 players.

However, there is no law governing the number of substitutions permitted in a contest. Actually this is a *rule* that the Fédération Internationale de Football Association (FIFA)—the sport's international governing body—insists be applied at the professional level. Because it is a rule and not a law, some discretion is involved at the amateur level, except for official international competitions such as the Summer Olympic Games.

For example, there is no limit to the number of subs that a college team may use. Players removed may later be reinstated. Under National Collegiate Athletic Association (NCAA) guidelines, any number of substitions are possible by either team whenever the ball crosses over the goal line.

In most high-school leagues, changes may also occur when the team making the substition(s) has a throw-in. Generally, if a player is shown the yellow card, or is shaken up, his coach can remove him from the game. Should he choose to do so, the other side is also allowed one change.

Remember that because this is a rule, substitution standards may vary from state to state, or even from county to county. As far as I know, in all leagues a player may not enter a game without the consent of the referee. However, some informal recreation programs permit changes as the action continues!

Teams may remove an injured player from action at any time, although his sub is not allowed in until play stops *and* the ref gives permission. It is up to the hurt player to leave the field under his own power or wait until play stops. In soccer, especially at the higher levels of the game, the action doesn't stop for an injury unless it requires immediate emergency medical attention. In fact, it's not uncommon to see a game progressing around a fallen athlete.

If an injured player is unable to leave the field, but it is not an emergency, the referee will generally halt play only when the injured player's team gains control of the ball and no scoring threat is imminent. Many times, a side will intentionally kick the ball out of bounds to stop play in such incidents.

**Ball Laws**—For a ball to be considered out of bounds, the entire ball must cross over the entire line. The position of the player in possession is irrelevant. You may control the ball with your feet—called *dribbling*—while you are outside the sideline, but the ball must be either on or inside the line. Furthermore, a ball need not touch the ground to be considered out of play. All lines extend upward in an imaginary vertical plane.

Likewise, for a goal to be awarded, the entire ball must cross the entire goal line. If the

Goalkeepers have to be quick, agile and very brave. (Jann Zlotkin)

goalie makes a save while he is in the goal but any portion of the ball is not, no score results.

As you advance in soccer, you'll discover that there are many little regulations and tricks of the trade to influence matches. For now, however, these basics are all you really need to know.

**Players' Roles**—Every coach allocates his 11 athletes somewhat differently. However, all sides include a goalkeeper. His primary responsibility is to prevent the ball from entering the net. A good goalie has outstanding hand-eye coordination, balance, acrobatic ability, reactions and courage. To anticipate action, a goalie must have a keen analytical mind and good knowledge of the game.

As he advances up the ranks, a goalie's role increases. By the time he's reached his mid-teens, a goalie should assume the responsibility of directing the team's defense. He is the only player who can see the entire field. As such, he must provide his teammates with useful advice such as telling them where an unguarded attacker is positioned.

A goalie's role is not entirely defensive. When he catches the ball, he must get it to a teammate. At that point he is transformed from the last defender to the first attacker. His ability to throw or kick the ball accurately plays a major role in successfully converting his side from defense to offense.

Helping the goalie to thwart attacks from the opposition are his *defenders*. Most teams use four defenders, although some use as many as five or as few as three.

As the name implies, a defender must guard—or *mark*—the other team's attackers. It is his job to prevent them from creating scoring opportunities. A good defender must be strong, quick, able to win balls in the air and on the ground, and not afraid to absorb a kick to clear the ball. He must have the skill to do something constructive with the ball when he gets it. This last aspect is sometimes overlooked by youth coaches. However, at more advanced levels of the game in modern soccer, *all* players must have good ball skills. Defenders are no exception to the rule!

Players in the middle of the field are understandably called *midfielders*. I think that midfielders have the most important role on the field. I know because I am one! Of course, plenty of folks contest that opinion—such as forwards, goalies and defenders!

A midfielder's tasks are both offensive and defensive. When his team has the ball, he supplies the skill and brains to coordinate the attack, mainly through passing. Exceptional midfielders are scoring threats too. My ex-teammate, Teofilo "Nene" Cubillas of Peru, is among the all-time leading scorers in World Cup history and is his nation's top scorer in that competition. This shows that a talented midfielder can be every bit as much a scoring threat as a *forward,* discussed soon.

Defensively, midfielders must get into good positions to slow down or halt the other team's advances. As such, they must be as adept at *tackling*—challenging a player with the ball for possession—as at passing, and as good at marking as at shooting. They must be fit enough to constantly move to the correct spot to do whatever is necessary.

The *forwards* are soccer's attackers. They don't require all-around attributes like midfielders, but they are the most frequent goalmakers. Even with a good attacking midfielder who is a scoring threat, the bulk of any team's firepower must come from its forwards to be consistently successful.

Obviously, a forward will receive plenty of attention from the opposition defense. He must have the quickness and dribbling skills to get away from markers, the power to win the ball in one-on-one confrontations and good control to *slot* the ball into the net.

To be a good goal scorer requires anticipation, judgment, courage and a wide variety of techniques. A truly exceptional forward is worth his weight in gold—or a lot more, judging by today's professional salaries.

The center forward, also called the striker, is the player whose ability to score is critical.

**Summary**—The beauty of soccer is that all players, regardless of position, must possess a wide range of skills. During the course of a match there will be many situations in which forwards must defend and defenders must attack.

Soccer is a flowing game without restrictions on players' mobility. In American football, an offensive tackle is ineligible to catch a forward pass. In *my* football, everyone can make or receive a pass, and we all have a chance to score. Maybe that's what makes soccer exhilarating.

Another admirable aspect of the sport is each athlete's decision-making responsibility. With 21 other players and so much space, possibilities for movements and passing sequences are endless. Each player must decide what to do both when in possession of the ball and when without it. There can be no greater feeling of satisfaction in team sports than when a group of people, thinking as individuals, move well collectively.

Good soccer can be as graceful as good dancing. Like the arts, it is a way of life for many lucky people. It can be the same for you, too, perhaps.

Whether you are a coach, a recreational player, or eventually reach the pros, the most important thing is to enjoy soccer. The best way to do that is to love the game, play for a team and a coach who try to win but don't consider victory as everything, and strive to become the best player you can be.

Along that road, you will experience many highs and lows. Keep your perspective—whether you win or lose, play well or play poorly, are cheered or booed. Count yourself as extremely fortunate to have the opportunity to compete. Remember that the beauty of sport is in the friendships we form and the lessons we're taught. Be thankful for your health and the ability to enhance it through soccer.

And remember that the bottom line is simple—have fun!

# CHAPTER TWO

# Trapping & Ball Control

All soccer skills are important, but the most important is ball control. Making the ball do precisely what you want as quickly as possible is the foundation of all other soccer skills. Except for rare *first-touch* shots, you cannot score if you haven't first controlled the ball. All great players I've faced have well-rounded skills, but they aren't great in all of them.

Péle, as talented as he was, was not the greatest passer of all time. Franz Beckenbauer, surely a soccer genius, was only an average scorer. George Best, the masterful dribbler, was an ordinary defensive player. But they were all great masters of ball control! This illustrates just how vital a skill it is. I don't know of any great players who didn't control a ball superbly. In most cases, it was what they did best.

## TRAPPING

Though each body part you use to first meet the ball requires a different technique, certain basics are common in all forms of *trapping*.

First, think of the ball as an egg. If I tossed you an egg, you'd naturally place your hands in front of your body and then pull them back softly when making the catch. You'd

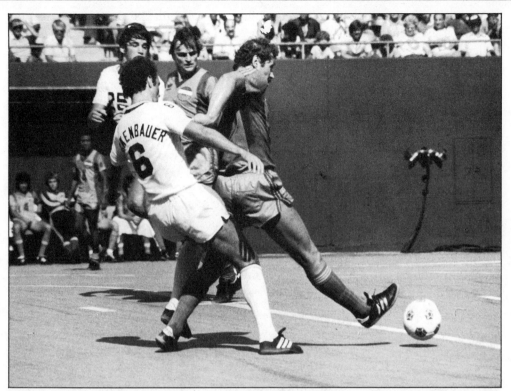

Perfect receiving technique. Notice how the attacker (dark jersey) uses his body as a legal shield while playing the ball in front of him. The defender is unable to reach it. (Stan Green)

do that instinctively so as not to crack the fragile shell.

Even though a soccer ball won't crack on contact, it will bounce away if met hard. The faster it's moving, the more gently you must trap it. This principle applies whether you meet the ball with your foot, thigh, chest, head or any other body part.

Second, you need good balance. Use your arms to enhance your balance, if need be, and always be prepared to move in any direction to receive the ball. The ball doesn't always arrive neatly. As often as not, it takes a bad bounce or deflects off someone at the last instant. Only if you're properly balanced can you react and trap well.

Third, concentration is critical. You must watch the ball—and the action—intently when you have to make a play.

Fourth is what I call the *Fast-Play Principle*. Whenever possible, meet the ball with the body part that is closest to the ground. A foot trap is preferable to a thigh trap, which is better than a chest trap, which is superior to a head trap. The lower the body part, the easier it is for you to be balanced as the ball touches the ground. In addition, the less distance the ball must travel to reach your feet, the less time it takes you to move with it or pass it.

You're also less predictable when controlling the ball with your feet. You have more options. The defender must, therefore, give you more room to turn, making your job easier.

Whenever I have a choice between standing my ground and executing a chest trap or taking a backward step to perform a thigh trap, I'll always opt for the latter. You'll discover that lower body parts make it easier to control the ball, even in isolated situations without defenders.

I've been told by fans and writers that I seem to bring the ball under control effortlessly. It may *look* that way from the stands, but, believe me, years of practice back up every trap.

There is precious little margin for error when trapping, especially at advanced levels of the game. That fact was dramatically demonstrated when my Strikers visited Giants' Stadium to challenge the Cosmos a few seasons ago. Midway through the game a high cross pass sailed through the Cosmos' penalty area, where Beckenbauer was perfectly positioned. Instinctively, I ran to close him down, fully prepared to pounce on the ball as soon as he brought it to the turf. In fact, in my mind's eye I had already decided in what corner of the goal my subsequent shot was going to enter.

The incomparable Franz Beckenbauer showing how a "defensive player" like a sweeper can be an offensive weapon too. (Stan Green)

Instead, Beckenbauer used his chest to flick the ball behind me, in a space where only he could reach it in a single stride. Before I could react, the greatest defender of all time was dribbling the ball toward our goal!

With almost any other opponent, even at the NASL level, my hustle would have been rewarded with a scoring opportunity. Not, however, with the "Kaiser." It was a reminder of something I mentioned before—the greatest players have the greatest ball control.

## FOOT TRAP

This is the most common and easiest trap. When you do it correctly, you can play the ball in one continuous motion. There are two commonly used varieties of foot traps. One involves the bottom of your shoe. The other uses the side.

When your back is to an opponent and the ball is rolling toward you, you'll want to keep it from the opponent. Using your upper body as a legal shield, control the ball with the bottom of the foot that is farther from the defender.

**FOOT TRAP**
Use the bottom of your foot to control a ball when the defender is directly behind you. (Jim Frank)

As you do this, lean backward so that you can literally feel his body touching yours. Doing this enables you to know where he's positioned without having to take your eyes off the ball.

Angle your shoe so that your toes are approximately level with the top of the ball and your heel is behind its middle. As the ball arrives, your foot steps down lightly onto the ball to "deaden" it. Be sure your touch is gentle. Don't smash the ball into the ground.

When the ball is moving toward you and the defender is to your front or side, use the inside of your shoe. On occasions when the ball arrives from a sharp angle on the side of your trapping foot, the outside of your shoe may be used. In all other cases, point your *supporting*—non-kicking—foot in the direction of the incoming pass. Place your trapping foot in front of your body. Your foot should be perpendicular to the direction of the pass, with the inside of your shoe exposed. Bend your knee slightly and have your weight forward.

As you feel the ball meet your foot, withdraw it so the ball comes to rest where you can move it in any direction with either foot. Doing so "freezes" the defender. He can't commit himself because he sees that you're threatening to advance toward any space he uncovers.

In contrast, if you bring the ball to rest on the outside of your right foot, an opponent knows it will take a series of time-consuming movements before you're able to advance the ball to your left. Therefore, he can position himself on your right side, effectively stopping you.

Incidentally, there is a third form of foot trap. But it's rare and is used only by advanced players. Should the ball be flying directly toward you, you can use your instep to "catch" it in midair before cradling it to the ground. Your knee must be bent, your body muscles relaxed to absorb the ball's force, and your foot must withdraw on impact.

## THIGH TRAP

Your entire upper leg, beginning just a few inches above your knee, may be used to bring the ball under control. As you begin your motion, you should be standing on the ball of your supporting foot. Once again, be loose. The more relaxed your body, the more relaxed the ball will be.

Bend your trapping leg from the knee and angle your upper leg so it is approximately perpendicular to the ball's line of flight. In other words, if the ball is descending directly downward, your upper leg should be parallel to the ground. If the ball is approaching on a line drive, your leg should be perpendicular to the turf.

Usually, the ball will travel between these two extremes. Your leg will normally have to be at an approximate 45° angle. No matter what the angle, you want to use the fleshy, upper side of your leg. Be careful not to let the ball hit your knee. If it does, it will bounce away.

As the ball meets your leg, pull your knee back and downward. With plenty of practice you should be able to drop the ball where it can immediately be played by either foot.

**THIGH TRAP**

Former Ohio Wesleyan All-American Billy Kohlasch shows how to use a thigh trap to pass the ball on the fly — also called a *volley* — to a nearby teammate. (Jim Frank)

With the thigh trap—and traps using the upper body—balance is harder to obtain than with the foot trap. It is important to judge just where the ball will arrive so you can play it without having to lunge. Don't set your feet prematurely, especially on windy days. The ball must be directly in front of your receiving limb or body part if you are to be properly balanced.

Don't hesitate to *look* awkward, if necessary, to get the job done. Like many pros, I use my hands and arms to improve balance. Sure, I may look silly, but not nearly as foolish as if I failed to control the ball. You get points for style in gymnastics. In soccer, results are all that count.

## CHEST TRAP

There are two forms of chest traps. One involves leaning forward and over a ball bouncing upward. The other requires you to lean backward from the waist to control a descending ball.

The first is often used while running, to avoid having to stop to master the ball. Once again, the angle of your upper body depends on the ball's line of flight. If you draw an imaginary line to represent the ball's path, it should form a 90° angle with your chest.

Don't worry about being gentle with this trap because the ball won't be moving too rapidly to make delicacy a problem. Besides, if you are moving full speed, there is no way to withdraw your body on impact even if you wanted too.

However, delicacy is important on the second type of chest trap—when the ball is descending. So, too, is proper pre-trap alignment. Position your body so the ball will arrive at the center of your chest, *not* to either side. As always, balance is vital.

What makes balance such a difficult proposition is that you must lean backward from the waist so your center of gravity is behind your feet. However, don't be flat-footed, if possible. Instead, stand on the balls of your feet.

To aid balance, place your arms outward. In addition, I find it helpful to take a deep breath before the ball arrives. Exhale as the ball makes contact. This cushions the blow and helps relax you during the trap.

As the ball descends and meets your chest, it should bounce just in front of your body. Quickly straighten your frame and lean forward so you're ready to play the ball before the defender can challenge for possession.

**RISING-BALL CHEST TRAP**
When performing a chest trap on a ball that's rising, lean over it so it will land in front of your feet. (Jim Frank)

**FALLING-BALL CHEST TRAP**
If the ball is descending, lean back and provide a cushion so it will land near your feet. Notice how you can use your arms to help balance. (Dan Herbst)

### HEAD TRAP

The rarest, and toughest, of all traps involves using your head. Lean back from your waist and loosen your neck muscles as much as possible. Allow the ball to hit your forehead. Withdraw it on impact to cushion the blow and control the ball.

**HEAD TRAP**
This is one of soccer's most rarely used skills, the head trap. (Jim Frank)

## SPECIAL TRAPS AND TOUCHES

The higher the trap occurs on your body, the more time the ball takes to reach your feet. If an opponent is nearby, you may find that you've inadvertently performed a service for him—bringing the ball down only to have him steal it before you've regained your balance.

To avoid that embarrassment, you have a couple of options. One is to deflect the ball into the space behind him. Then you run into that space to get the ball. This uses his momentum against him. It's easier than trying to stop the ball on the ground. Of course, if you choose this option, he shouldn't be backed up by any teammates. Otherwise, they'll get the ball.

Another idea is to play the ball to a nearby teammate of yours *before* it hits the ground. Practice trapping the ball on your thigh and *volleying* it—hitting it in midair—with your instep. Keep your toes down to gain accuracy and keep the ball from sailing above your target.

With your marker moving to stop your progress—and perhaps neglecting to notice what is happening behind him—you have a perfect opportunity to start a passing sequence. Basically, you play the ball to a teammate, instantly sprint into open space behind your rival, and receive a return pass.

A final option is simply not to play the ball. If you're near the sideline, or if you have an open teammate in the direction that the ball is moving, why not pretend to play the ball only to step aside at the last instant. Your fake will "freeze" your marker.

Always consider your options. It is far better to not play a ball and concede a throw-in—for which your team will have time to set up defensively—than to put yourself out of the play by trapping incorrectly and losing the ball.

## SUMMARY

On all of these traps, you must *unlearn* a basic principle of most American team sports. It's important that you *do not* keep your eyes glued to the ball! As the ball arrives, get a quick survey of the field. A soccer field is a crowded place. Players are drawn to the ball. You can not afford the luxury of making a trap and then looking up to decide what to do. By that time you will be tightly marked and perhaps outnumbered.

Anticipation is the key, and that is helped by a good overview of the situation. Know what you want to do before touching the ball.

## BALL-CONTROL PRACTICE

Before long you'll have developed a mental checklist of what certain body movements do to the ball. If so, you're on your way to developing *touch,* that special feel for the ball that all great players possess.

**Juggling**—The most basic exercise to enhance this trait is to *juggle* the ball. Using all body parts except, of course, your hands and arms, try to keep the ball aloft for as many consecutive touches as you can. Challenge yourself.

I'll never forget the first time I achieved 10 straight touches. Few moments on a field since have given me as great a feeling of satisfaction as that experience.

As you improve, practice juggling using just one part of the body. Or, use only your right or left side. Or, work in patterns such as head to chest to thigh to instep and back to your head.

Of course, you probably will rarely juggle a ball in a match. What good does it do to practice a skill for hours that isn't match-related? You'll develop confidence in ball

**JUGGLING**
Practice it to develop ball mastery and better balance. (Dan Herbst)

control. You'll also improve your balance, a vital ingredient when you perform so many different soccer techniques. This comes from learning to touch the ball properly while standing on one foot as you juggle with the other.

Believe it or not, the University of Connecticut, home of one of the top collegiate soccer clubs in North America, requires all of its varsity players to pass a juggling test. It's the opinion of coach Joe Morrone that a player who can juggle the ball at least 50 consecutive times with his left foot can be relied on to make a proper 10-yard pass with that foot.

Juggling is a skill you can perform in tandem. Or a group of players can engage in games of *Keep It Up* to see how many touches they can accumulate before the ball hits the ground.

There are a number of juggling devices you can use, such as soft sacks or even tennis balls, to develop coordination. Though I wouldn't recommend spending countless hours with them, they can prove helpful in building some skills.

For you beginners who become frustrated, there is an alternative drill. Let the ball hit the ground between every touch. This will give you more time to get into the proper pre-kick position and balance. As your skill improves move up to the more challenging and more commonly used variety of juggling.

**Trapping**—Use a wall to substitute for teammates when none are to be found. Throw, or kick, the ball off the wall and then try to control it on the first touch. With your back to the wall, do the same before turning and moving into the ball's line of flight. Then execute the most appropriate trap.

**SOLO PRACTICE**
Alone, you can still have a good practice session by using a wall. (Jim Frank)

If a friend is present, have him feed balls of varying spins and from various locations to you. Work on all parts of your body and have your friend alternate targets. This simulates a game environment in which you never know in advance which skill you'll be called on to use. If two pals are around, have one serve you balls while the other challenges you for possession.

**Moving Drill**—The next step is to control balls as you're moving. One drill involves having a server 5 to 10 yards from the trapper. The latter jogs backward and is tossed balls. He must bring them under control on the first touch and volley a pass back into the server's hands on the second touch. Once again, take turns serving different types of tosses so that all parts and both right and left sides of the body are used.

**Head Tennis**—This is a popular game and exercise to develop ball control. It combines the skills of soccer with the rules of volleyball and tennis.

You play on a tennis court, wearing sneakers. The singles lines and service boxes serve as the area of play, with two or three persons on each team. A drop kick is used to serve the ball. Only the serving team may score a point. Should they lose the play, the other team begins the subsequent point by serving. Each team is limited to three touches per possession. The ball may touch the ground during play only once each time it goes over the net.

Head Tennis is great fun and helps improve your touch. (Jim Frank)

Although the game is called *Head Tennis,* you can touch the ball with *all* parts of your body except your hands and arms. And a tennis court is not essential. Almost any object, from a bench to a piece of string, can serve as your net.

Head Tennis is great fun and a tremendous developer of ball-control skills. Believe me, those Head Tennis tournaments that we hold at an occasional Striker practice can get very competitive. There's always plenty of good-natured kidding that promotes team spirit. For players possessing at least a modicum of skill, it's a great way to train.

**Summary**—Acquiring top-notch ball control requires two things. First, play in plenty of matches. These can be league or pick-up games, as long as the players are giving full effort. No practice setting, no matter how realistic, can fully simulate the pressure that you're subjected to in a game. Only real games force you to be at your sharpest.

Second, spend plenty of time alone with the ball. Ball control doesn't just happen. You don't wake up one morning to discover that you're a Beckenbauer, a Cruyff or a Péle. If you want to excel, you have to spend hundreds of hours playing with that ball. Juggle it. Try moves on imaginary opponents. Use a practice wall to full advantage.

There are no shortcuts to learning ball control. But if you can train yourself to master the ball, you'll have built the foundation that all great players used to become great.

# CHAPTER THREE

# Heading

There's one skill that brings shudders to the soccer novice—smashing your head into a soccer ball. I can't tell you how many times a fan has looked at me incredulously and asked, "Doesn't that hurt?" The answer is a qualified "No," but only if you use proper technique. It *will* hurt if you do not.

## BASIC TECHNIQUE

Pause for a second and run your fingers over your head. Now do it and apply modest pressure. It should be readily apparent that not all portions of your skull are equally hard. The front of your face and the top of your head are soft. A blow to either of those places is discomforting.

However, your forehead is both firm and flat. The part just below your hairline is ideally suited for redirecting a ball. This is called *heading*. To head the ball successfully, observe the following:

1) Do not close your eyes. Upon impact, they'll shut automatically. However, if you close them before contact, rather than watching the ball approach, the ball is likely to hit either your nose or the top of your skull. The greatest cause of such painful errors is fear of the ball, which becomes a self-fulfilling prophecy.

2) *You* must strike the ball; the ball shouldn't strike you. Your neck muscles should be rigid. As the ball approaches, lean back from your waist. With your entire upper body stiff, thrust forward from your waist and into the ball. This will impart needed power.

Right: Heading is one of soccer's most important, and exciting, skills. (Milt Crossen)

3) As with putting a golf ball, eliminate all superfluous movements. Despite the bending from the waist and the subsequent head thrust, the only head motion is short and snappy. From coil to conclusion of follow-through, no more than a couple feet are covered.

**HEADING**
You power the ball by thrusting your entire upper body into and through the ball. Your neck remains rigid. (Jim Frank)

## WHEN TO HEAD

There are three basic situations in which you perform a header—defensively, offensively to pass the ball, and when you have a shot at goal.

**Defensive Header**—This often occurs in or near your own penalty area. There, it's necessary to propel the ball high and far. It's your objective to move the ball a great distance from your own goal.

To impart height on your clearance, hit just under the center of the ball. You'll want to make contact as you're still rising, just before the apex of your leap.

One important tip: You'll probably perform the defensive header in heavy traffic, so you may be jostled as you jump. If so, don't leap straight upward. Instead, begin your jump behind where you intend to head the ball. Leap forward and upward. This will also increase the force imparted to the ball.

**Offensive Header**—The second situation finds you somewhere in the middle of the field, possibly with a bit more time and space. In this situation, you want your team to maintain possession after the header. If you wish to pass to someone nearby, you'll need to absorb the ball's pace. After all, you want your pass to be easy for a teammate to control and not too hard and fast. This strategy is often used on throw-ins where the receiver "nods" the ball back to the unmarked thrower.

To nod the ball, *do not* move your head into the ball. This is one exception to the second rule I discussed earlier. Instead, ready yourself as usual, but let the ball hit your forehead. As always during a header, keep your upper body and neck rigid.

If the pass must cover a greater distance, combine the technique just described with that of the defensive header. This aids accuracy. Remember that the lower on the ball your forehead hits, the higher the ball will fly. This is not advantageous when passing because the longer the pass takes to arrive, the less time and space the receiver will have to control it.

**Scoring Header**—This is by far the toughest. As with any loose ball in the penalty area, you can be sure you'll be challenged for possession. You must head it downward with both accuracy and power. This isn't easy because you usually have to redirect the ball's path.

It's important to head the ball downward. Ideally, it should pass by the goalie as it is bouncing. It's the toughest save for a goalie to make. That's because he is usually upright, having set himself for a high cross.

Time your leap so you are above the ball's line of flight. Strike above the center of the ball and snap your head forward and down.

If the ball comes from a sideline, you may not be able to use the middle of your forehead. You may have to hit the ball with the scalp above the eye that is closer to the goal line. This is referred to as a *flick header*. It is especially effective on corner kicks and long throw-ins.

Another variety that's helpful near the opposition goal is the *back header*. In general,

Ray Hudson using his head to score a goal. Note how Ray moves toward the ball and jumps high to head it downward, the toughest place for a goalie to make the save. (Jim Frank)

it's used by an attacker who is stationed at the side of the goal. It is used to send the ball across the face of the net.

Hit the underside of the ball with the top of your forehead. To add height, tuck your chin against your chest as the ball arrives and flick the ball upward. You'll find that by running to the ball you will draw defenders out of the danger zone in front of their goal. This leaves space for your teammates to move in as the ball arrives.

You've no doubt guessed that flick and back headers are easier said than done. In fact, the mere act of heading a ball is so far removed from any skill utilized in other popular American sports that you'll probably take longer to become proficient in it than with any other soccer skill.

Don't be discouraged. More important, don't be intimidated. Fear of the ball is likely to result in a painful experience. You must head the ball aggressively. Concentrate on keeping your eyes open and watching the ball until it lands on your forehead. This way you will avoid that unpleasant experience of having the ball bash your nose or scalp.

**SOLO PRACTICE**
Here's a good way to practice heading by yourself. (Jim Frank)

## HEADING PRACTICE

Learning how to head is twice as tough as most other soccer skills because it involves two factors—developing proper technique *and* overcoming fear. The latter is no small consideration. If you miskick an instep drive, for example, there is only the "pain" of embarrassment. Mishead a ball, however, and you can end up with a first-class headache.

**Beginning**—To avoid headaches, start with this simple procedure. Hold the ball in front of your forehead with your hands to the sides and at the far end of the ball. At the same time, bring the ball back to meet your head as your forehead snaps forward to strike the ball.

The next step is to gently toss the ball onto your head and head it back into your hands. You'll soon discover that heading is painless when technique is correct.

**Next Phase**—Have a friend flip underhand tosses from 5 to 10 yards for you to head. Have him serve some high balls to encourage you to leap a bit. If you're still afraid of the ball, remove some air to make it softer.

**PARTNER PRACTICE**
As you get better, have a partner flip balls for you to head. (Jim Frank)

You must develop the feel of thrusting your entire upper body to meet the ball. One good way to learn this is to kneel. Lean backward as a friend flips a ball toward your head. As it arrives, thrust forward and smash your forehead into the ball. Keep your eyes open!

Then go back to the preceding drill. This time, have your friend toss balls from a greater distance. Concentrate on good technique and meet the ball aggressively.

**KNEELING PRACTICE**
This kneeling drill will help you learn to thrust your upper body forward as you head the ball. (Jim Frank)

**Suspended Ball**—Another popular drill uses a ball suspended on a string from an overhead object such as a tree branch. Leap up and head the ball. Practice jumping off either foot and off both feet. Remember, in a match you may not always have time to leap off the stronger foot. You need to train as you expect to play, being prepared for whatever situations a match might present.

**CAUTION**

There is one type of header that I've intentionally neglected until now. That's the *diving header*.

It's best left to physically mature players who possess plenty of skill, savvy and courage. It can be a great offensive and defensive weapon, but only in the arsenal of an athlete who has the tools to use it correctly. To everyone else, it's merely dangerous.

The diving header is used when the airborne ball arrives low and in front. You must time your dive so your entire body is parallel to the ground as you meet the ball. Once again, your neck is rigid, your eyes are open and your hairline contacts the ball. Place your hands in front of you, palms downward, to help cushion your landing.

For those first attempting this maneuver, try to find a soft surface. A sandy beach or gym mat is ideal.

While the diving header can be spectacular, and certainly effective, it is also rare. Once again, for all but the most advanced players, it's not necessary and can be dangerous.

Instead, concentrate on sharpening the fundamentals—keep your eyes open; contact the middle of the ball (most of the time); meet the ball with your hairline; and thrust your upper body forward, with neck rigid, into the ball.

**DIVING HEADER**
This is certainly not a technique for beginners or the faint of heart. (Jim Frank)

# CHAPTER FOUR

# Dribbling

There are few sights in sports as exciting as watching an attacker in full flight take on a defender one-on-one. As the attacker moves the ball with his feet—called *dribbling*—excitement spreads throughout the stadium. With the exception of a goal, nothing thrills soccer fans as much. They know that something exceptional will be forthcoming. More often than not, they are right.

To a player, these match-ups provide the great stimulation of an individual challenge—man against man—within a team-structured game. Trying to move with the ball around an opponent, or attempting to prevent someone from doing that to you, is one of the enjoyable and essential parts of soccer.

When I was growing up in England, George Best was considered the master. His ability to dribble through entire teams was legendary. As a pro, I witnessed his incredible skill firsthand. We were playing in San Jose and leading 2-0 when the great one went to work. Taking the ball on a pass just after a kickoff, Best dribbled around several of my teammates, literally turning our last defender completely around in the penalty area. He then shot the ball into the net with such ease that it seemed as if he were a man playing against boys.

Sparked by this great play, a subsequent goal and assist by Best enabled the Earthquakes to beat us 3-2 that night. Best's score, which earned him the 1981 NASL Goal of the Year honors, was proclaimed by many experts as the greatest tally in the history of the league. As an unhappy witness to that feat, I can't quarrel with their assessment.

Next to goal-scoring, dribbling is soccer's most exciting skill. (Stan Green)

## WHY DRIBBLE?

It's fitting that a score created by superb dribbling technique thrills people most. In a sport that is a joint effort among 11 players, a dash of individual brilliance is special. Because dribbling is the essence of soccer, it provides an opportunity for a player to express his skill, flair and creativity.

The way the game is played today, with many teams using so many players in defensive roles, great dribblers are more valuable than ever before. When penalty areas are packed, conventional — and predictable — passes are rarely sufficient to break down the defense. It's then that something extra is needed. At times, it seems that dribbling is becoming a lost art in modern soccer.

If you examine the rosters of great teams at any level, it's amazing how often the presence of one or more great dribblers can be found. That's no coincidence. Yet, this extraordinarily valuable breed of player is almost an endangered species.

The reason, I fear, is coaching. Or, rather, over-coaching. When a young player loses a ball in a match, too often his coach becomes visibly and audibly upset. "Why didn't you pass the ball?" is a common response.

Somehow, dribbling has become equated with selfishness, as if the player wants to keep the ball for himself. Sure, there are athletes who can be accused of such transgressions. But many others possess special gifts that, if encouraged, can be harnessed to great advantage.

If you're a youth coach, I implore you to encourage your charges to experiment and take chances. Only through trial and error will they improve.

Of course, there are times when dribbling isn't appropriate. Certainly, you shouldn't ever lose the ball by dribbling it in your own half of the field. It's usually best to pass it upfield to an open teammate. This is especially true around your own penalty area. And you shouldn't keep the ball when you have an open teammate nearby who is available for a pass. Nothing is a greater cause of team dissension than such selfishness.

**DRIBBLING**
1) Here's Rick Davis, U.S. National Team captain, dribbling around a defender. Notice how Rick keeps his head up as he moves forward. Always dribble with your head up so you can spot open teammates.

Having said that, I must stress that dribbling is a great way to dissect a defense. The next time you see an exceptional ball master in action, notice what effect his actions have on the opposing team. You'll see that markers are drawn to him like moths to light. Before long, he is greatly outnumbered simply because the danger posed by his skills is so great.

When exploited to the fullest, this presents the offensive player with two very good options: If he feels confident, he can take those players on and beat them. Or, he can pass the ball, having created space for his side by pulling defenders toward him and away from other attackers. If the dribbler is near the touchline, his magnetism may result in the defense's being understaffed in the middle, where potential scorers now have more time and space to operate. Either way, dribbling is a threatening weapon.

## WHAT YOU NEED

Over the years, as both fan and player, I've had the privilege of seeing some of the greatest dribblers of all time up close. There is no soccer skill that allows so much liberty for individual style. Some dribblers rely predominantly on finesse, while others depend on power. Some have lightning-quick moves; others depend on acceleration.

2) Then he changes direction, keeping the ball closer to his feet than the defender's. (Stan Green)

There are, however, certain common traits that you need to perform this skill effectively. Among these are exceptional mastery over the ball, good balance, the ability to deceive and the courage to withstand intimidation.

## HOW TO DRIBBLE

There are very few "rules" of dribbling. A chest trap, for example, features several components that you must execute properly to be consistently successful. Dribbling does not. There aren't set types of dribbles as there are traps.

So how can I teach dribbling in a book? Rather than try to describe the fluid moves that a great dribbler might use, I prefer to underscore the *principles* involved, as well as what you can do to develop good habits and skills.

**Control**—The first principle is that you must retain control of the ball and keep it closer to your feet than your marker's. If the ball "runs away" from you, your opponent will have little trouble initiating a successful *tackle*.

This sounds both obvious and easy. It isn't easy at all. It requires finesse and a deft touch while moving at or near full speed.

**Balance**—Another principle is to lean forward and over the ball as you are either faking a motion or dribbling around your opponent. The result is a low center of gravity, which promotes balance. This way you are able to change direction quickly. It's necessary because you often have to alter course quickly to counter defenders. A great dribbler like Best will often bend his knees so much that they seem to be scraping the top of the ball.

**BODY FAKING**
1) The attacker steps over the ball with his right foot and starts to lean left.

2) This draws the marker to that side, "wrong-footing" him.

3) The attacker then uses a quick touch of the ball with the outside of the right foot to move past the defender. (Jim Frank)

**Faking**—Great dribblers have the ability to "wrong foot" defenders. They can convince a defender that they're going in one direction and then move the opposite way as soon as the defender moves his body in the direction they had feinted toward.

For this, agile hips and shoulders come in very handy. While the defender *should* watch only the ball and your feet, he can often be fooled with clever upper-body movements. An act as simple as lowering your shoulder and leaning in that direction can often take a marker out of the play.

I've even seen eye fakes! A schoolboy teammate of mine would look to his right, point his hand toward an imaginary target, and yell "Go" to a non-existent teammate on that side. When the defender would move in that direction, my friend simply dribbled left. It was a "sucker" play, but it worked consistently.

**Decisiveness**—Know in advance where you want to go. Decide early where the most space is available and which spot leaves you with the best options. Having made that decision, utilize deception to convince your marker that you're going in the opposite direction of your intended destination.

Two can play the game. An advanced defender may feint as if to challenge for the ball only to back off just as quickly. It is his hope that you'll panic when he moves toward you and react to his feint by exposing the ball. When this happens, the winner will be decided by your respective skill levels. The greater your mastery of the ball—and your ability to recover—the better the odds are in your favor.

**Physical Strength** — Physical components also come into the equation. Strength is a definite asset. As you move around a foe, you can expect a hearty challenge. Often this means a legal shoulder-to-shoulder charge. If he's able to overpower you, all of your superior skill will go for naught. You need not be built like Mr. Universe to prevail. But you players in high school, and beyond, should have done some work in the weight room, if needed, to ensure you've reached a minimum acceptable level of strength.

**Mental Strength** — This, too, is essential. Let's face it, no defender likes being beaten. As you progress in soccer, you'll find that more and more opponents will tackle whatever they can as you try to maneuver around them. If you've pushed the ball into a spot where they can't challenge for it, they may opt to "tackle" your shins instead.

Don't foolishly retaliate. Instead, brush yourself off and punish them the best way possible, by using skill to place the resulting free kick in the back of the net.

It's very important that you be able to withstand the rigors of overly aggressive defenders. The better your dribbling skills, the more of a marked man you'll become. For example, in the 1982 World Cup, the highly touted Diego Maradona was brutalized by Italy's ruthless centerback, Claudio Gentile. The referee did little to protect the Argentinian. Gentile's tactics, while not pretty to watch, were an extremely significant factor in his nation's winning the Cup. Nor was he at all repentant after the match. When asked about some of his tougher tackles, he replied simply, "It's not a dance contest!"

In other words, if the referee won't prohibit that "style" of defending, players like Gentile will do all they can, legal or otherwise, to help their team win. There are too few officials who are strict with such questionable challenges. Many give the tactic of intimidation an unfair edge over the application of skill.

There have been countless incidents of shameless brutality by defenders who would rather break an opponent's leg than concede a goal. Penalizing such play is an important priority for referees at all levels. And this surely applies to any volunteer youth-soccer officials reading this book. You must opt for safety and skill over injuries and intimidation.

**Bodywork**—Generally speaking, most fouls occur as one player passes another. Knowing that, you must be physically and mentally prepared for contact at such times. When you've made your move and are dribbling around your rival, position the ball on the outside of the foot that is farther from him. If contact appears likely, lean toward him and, if possible, lower your shoulder into his. This will impede his efforts to knock you off balance.

A very effective tool to aid your package of deception is a change of pace. Most great dribblers rarely sprint at their opponents. Generally, they operate at full speed only when their marker is the last defender between them and the goal. Usually plenty of space is available behind that defender. In most other cases, it is to your advantage to dribble at three-quarter speed.

To the defender, you still appear to be running rapidly. However, you still have an extra "gear" to use after making your final feint. Some of soccer's premier dribblers, such

Whenever possible, place the ball on the outside of the foot that is farther from the defender as you dribble around him. (Jim Frank)

as Brazil's famed Garrincha, seemed to be walking with the ball. As soon as the defender thought Garrincha had lost control, he would challenge for it. At that instant, Garrincha would pull the ball away from his man and accelerate by him as if the opponent were standing still.

Remember, you have an inherent advantage in a one-on-one situation where there is space behind your marker. If you push the ball into that gap, your rival must stop, turn and chase the ball from a standing start. You, in contrast, are already in full stride. If you slow him down further by slightly decreasing your speed, you make it easier on yourself to control the ball, while enhancing your opportunity to accelerate past him.

**Footwork**—There is another "hole" you can use. If the defender has his legs spread too far apart, which often happens to taller players who tend to have upright stances, slide the ball between his feet! As he closes his legs, dash around him and collect the ball on the other side. This is illustrated in an accompanying sequence of photos. In soccer lingo this is known as a *nutmeg*.

No matter what moves you use, you'll find that you can control the ball best by touching it with the portion of your shoe that covers the outside of either your largest or smallest toe. Don't use the front of your foot when taking an opponent on. The ball will just roll away from you.

Another option is to place the ball close to your rival and then pull it away by using the bottom of your foot. As a schoolboy, I marveled at Charlie Cooke's ability to do this. He was not unlike a matador waving a cape at the charging bull—only to withdraw it as the

**NUTMEG**
Use the "nutmeg" move to dribble the ball between a marker's legs. (Jim Frank)

animal flew harmlessly by. The principle is the same. Use an opponent's momentum against him. Just as the matador nearly always prevails, so, too, will the dribbler who is able to bait his defensive rival.

**FOOTWORK**
A good dribbler knows how to use the bottom of his feet to pull the ball away from the defender. (Jim Frank)

**Don't Relax**—After you've moved around your foe, your job is far from completed. Don't relax and think "I've got it made." It's important that you continue moving with the same sense of urgency and pace to put more space between you and him. Otherwise, you'll have to beat him again. Once is enough. Players who relax after beating a defender invite their opponent back into the play.

**Shielding**—Not all dribbling is intended to get past an opponent. There will be times, especially for strikers, when maintaining possession is your objective. Often a long pass is struck to a forward who receives the ball with his back to the opponents' goal. In this situation he is usually badly outnumbered with no open teammate nearby. Rather than turn and fruitlessly challenge several defenders, he should "hold" the ball until support arrives. In this case, he uses his body as a *shield,* a legal impediment that separates the ball from the defender.

To shield successfully do the following: First, place the ball under the foot that is farther from your defender. If he's on your right side, play the ball with your left foot. Second, use the underside of your foot to control the ball. This allows you to roll it from side to side to escape challenges. It also permits you to keep the ball a good distance from your body, out of the range of your defender's outstretched legs. You can also feel the ball the entire time, allowing you the luxury of not having to look at it as you maintain control.

**SHIELDING**
Notice how the young man in the dark jersey is using his arms to shield. In addition, he is using his far foot to execute his trap. (Jim Frank)

Third, you may use your arm to aid your shield but you are not allowed to swing it back into the defender. If it's in a natural position near your side, the referee should permit it. This widens the area of your shield. Your opponent now has farther to move to get to the ball. Once again, strength is an asset. You may lean into your defender, and you can be sure that a strong one will be leaning onto you. Leverage through a lower center of gravity can make you seem "stronger" than you really are. No good striker can survive if he doesn't have good physical strength. Shielding certainly requires that.

## DRIBBLING PRACTICE

Now that I've covered the basic principles of dribbling, let's look at some of the practice drills, exercises and games you should pursue to develop the skill.

I have some good news for you players who hate to train. There are many dribbling games that will do wonders for your skill and are great fun as well. Just as dribbling is one of soccer's true joys, so is the one-on-one challenge during practice sessions. Next to shooting, it's probably the skill that players enjoy honing most. It is certainly one that they'll find invaluable as they progress up the soccer ladder.

**Smart Feet**—The first step is to develop a sense of touch. Your feet must become "knowledgeable," learning how to make contact with the ball to produce the desired result.

To start, place the ball between your feet and, while standing on your toes, tap the ball from one foot to the other using only the inside of your shoes. As you progress, perform the same skill while moving. Another advanced variation is to do it while rotating your body.

Next, place the ball in front of you. Using the sole of your shoe, tap the ball with your right foot, then your left. Alternate feet as you hop on your supporting foot. As you improve, you should be able to touch the ball consistently without moving it. Challenge yourself as you progress by performing this drill without looking at the ball, then by circling around it. Once you've mastered that, find a partner.

**Partner Practice**—With the stationary ball between you, touch it simultaneously with your right feet and then with your left. Once again, the ball should not move and you will, in time, be able to rotate around the ball without having to look at it.

You may wonder why you shouldn't look at the ball. In a game, it's vital that you be able to dribble with your head up. A good dribbler not only has the skill to maneuver around opponents, but he also possesses good soccer vision, being able to control the ball while scanning the field to search for open teammates and space. If you have to look at the ball to control it, you won't be able to tell what your marker is doing or where other opponents are. Without that information, you'll probably be caught doing the wrong thing at the wrong time and in the wrong place.

**Moving Practice**—Another dribbling drill used to upgrade skill and vision is to jog forward while pushing the ball slightly ahead of you with the bottom of your feet. You can do this with only your right or left foot, or by alternating feet. Either way, don't let the

**PARTNER PRACTICE**
When practicing dribbling with a partner, try not to look at the ball. Be gentle so it won't move as your feet strike it. (Jim Frank)

ball get too far in front of you, where an imaginary defender could steal it. Move with short, but quick, strides and touch the ball with every step.

Although these drills are basic, they provide good warm-up exercises, even for advanced players. You're never too good to spend a few moments practicing with the ball. If you were to wander into our locker room before a match, you'd find many players juggling, hitting balls off the wall and performing simple passes with teammates. Even at our level, such moments are very helpful. A fundamentally sound player achieves that status by mastering the basics. That can be achieved only through repetition.

## DRIBBLING GAMES

Dribbling is the ultimate one-on-one skill. It's player against player, and may the better player win. One of the most popular games, especially at the youth level, is to advance through a series of cones, slalom-style. The cones can be close together or far apart, depending on your skill. Try this using a variety of touches—with both feet, with only the insides of both feet, with only the outsides of both feet, with only your left foot, with only your right foot and with the bottoms of your feet.

When an entire team is practicing, the coach can divide his squad and have relay races. To simulate a game setting with the better players, add extra conditions. For example, on hearing the coach's whistle, players dribbling must stop the ball using a specific body part, such as a forehead or knee. Not only will this provide some laughs for all, it will prevent participants from pushing the ball too far ahead of them. This forces them to maintain close control of the ball, just as they must do when tightly marked in a match.

**Heads-Up Practice**—Another important component of dribbling technique is to advance the ball while looking ahead. To teach this, the coach can position himself between the two lines of cones. When he raises his arm, the dribblers may skip the remaining cones and pass the ball to the next player in line. Teammates are not allowed to tell the dribbler when the coach's hand is raised.

**Winterbottoms**—This is my favorite one-on-one game. To play, you need six people. At any one time, two players serve as the goals (by spreading their legs beyond shoulder width), two as retrievers and two as participants. The object is to dribble around your rival and push-pass the ball into his goal.

The persons serving as the goals each have a ball. Should the ball in play be kicked over the imaginary goal line, the "goal" puts in a new ball. This way, there is constant action. It's the retrievers' job to keep the persons serving as goals supplied with balls at all times.

A few minutes of Winterbottoms is a full workout. Play in 60-second intervals and keep a score for the entire game, which can consist of any number of "periods."

This drill is also good practice for honing your jockeying and tackling abilities. These are covered in chapter 7.

**Buffalo Stampede**—This is a real favorite among the younger set. It's played in a grid, about 20 to 30 yards long and 15 to 25 yards wide. The size depends on the athletes' skill—smaller for more advanced players—and the number of participants—the more people, the more space required.

All players except one stand on one of the goal lines, each with a ball. On signal, they must dribble from that goal line to the other. The extra player is a defender. It's his task to either steal balls or kick them out of bounds. When that occurs, the players losing their balls become defenders on subsequent rushes. Eventually, defenders will outnumber attackers, providing a real challenge for the remaining offensive players. The winner is the last attacker in possession of his ball.

Extra conditions may be placed on advanced players to hone their skills, such as dribbling only with their weaker foot.

Field markings may also be added to improve dribbling skills. With young players, it's a challenge to dribble a ball along a line.

**Center-Circle Games**—The best segment of the field for teaching dribbling is the center circle. There are two games, in particular, that I heartily endorse.

*Crab Soccer* involves an approximate 2:1 ratio of dribblers to defenders. All are in the center circle with each attacker dribbling his own ball in the circle. The defenders try to dispossess the attackers and kick their balls outside the circle. There is, however, one catch. The defenders must maneuver with both feet and hands on the turf.

When an attacker loses his ball, one of two things can happen. Either he exchanges places with the defender who won it from him or he is out of the game. If you use the

**CRAB SOCCER**
This is a fun game for improving dribbling skills. (Jim Frank)

second option, the winner is the last player with his ball.

A variation on the same theme is known as *Center-Circle Kickout.* In this game, every player has his own ball. The objective is to maintain possession while knocking the balls of other players outside of the circle.

When that happens, the player losing his ball is out of the game. As the number of participants dwindles, the playing area can be decreased. After all, a good dribbler must be able to operate in confined quarters.

You coaches will soon discover which of your players possess a keen analytical soccer mind. By the second or third practice game, your smarter athletes will have discovered that, in Center-Circle Kickout at least, discretion is the better part of valor. They will "hide," staying away from the action. Let others knock each other out, they'll think; I'll just wait here until most of them are eliminated.

Though the logic is irrefutable, their course of action will do little to develop their skills. To prevent that, add two ingredients.

First, institute a rule that the players must keep the balls moving at all times. This forces them to dribble. By doing so, they will develop their skill as well as an awareness of moving toward open space.

A second stipulation is that players eliminated from the action may re-enter the game when the person who got them out is, in turn, knocked out. Therefore, to win the game a player must eventually eliminate all of his rivals. This condition has two positive features. Obviously, it encourages players to take risks, forcing them to build technique and judgment. It also keeps those outside the circle involved with the action, cheering for their teammates to "get so-and-so." This is far better than having them bored and discouraged—especially with younger children who have shorter attention spans.

The best aspect of this game is that it demands many of the technical *and* tactical skills necessary in match situations. At first, you may tackle recklessly. When that occurs, you'll find that, while you're challenging someone else, a third party has sneaked behind you to kick your ball away. In short order, you'll learn to feint and to be aware of what's happening all around you. Developing 360° vision—knowing what is behind and in front—is a key ingredient in making you a complete player.

**CENTER-CIRCLE KICKOUT**
This game requires almost all of the physical *and* mental skills you'll need to dribble effectively in a game. (Jim Frank)

But the thing I like most about Center-Circle Kickout is that it's so much fun. From the sandlots to the stadium, from youth to adults, it's a great game to play.

**Follow The Leader**—This is another fun practice game, especially for beginning players. Players take turns being the leader, performing various dribbling moves. All others must watch him and duplicate his movements. Once again, you're required to perform various touches of the ball. Coaches should encourage players to do this without looking at the ball.

**Simple Simon**—Try this old game. Use the standard rules, such as, "Simon says dribble in a circle. . ."

As you can see, there are plenty of dribbling games that are both fun and productive. The best are those that include elements of opposition, limited time and space, decision-making and the execution of the skill itself. For that reason, games like Crab Soccer and Center-Circle Kickout are highly recommended.

# CHAPTER FIVE

# Passing

All great teams are able to frequently maintain possession of the ball through a series of accurate, well-executed passes. When done right, it looks simple. But look closer. You'll see that in every correct pass is a player who is concentrating 100% on the task at hand—or should I say foot?

Believe me, there is no such thing as an "easy" pass. I've seen far too many games lost by a player who was needlessly casual when executing a "simple" pass. Too often the ball is intercepted and shot into his team's net.

Yet, most passes do not require the refined touch of, say example, a 20-yard shot. Nine times out of ten, passing involves nothing more than sound judgment and proper execution of basic techniques. However, to perform consistently well, you need to develop good habits early.

## CONCENTRATION

When passing, never take anything for granted. When making a 10-yard pass, it's an easy temptation to stab at the ball rather than smoothly stroking it. Outstanding passers use a sharp address on the ball coupled with a smooth touch. That comes only through years of practice in which they prided themselves on stroking the ball perfectly. A five-yard pass must be hit with the same urgency and determination as a 40-yard pass. If it isn't you'll find there's an alert opponent waiting to pounce on your lazy effort.

## CONSIDERATION

A second component, also often neglected, is what I term *consideration*. Most passers think only of how they can deliver the ball to a teammate. An equally vital factor is what he can do with the ball after he gets it. If he has a defender on his left side, you should pass to his right. If he's wide open, place the ball ahead of him so he can collect it on the run toward the opponents' goal. If he's tightly marked, give him a *service*—a pass—that's easy to control instantly. Or, perhaps, you should simply look to pass somewhere else.

Consider your teammate's attributes and liabilities. If he's not a skillful player, passing him the ball when he's in traffic is *not* a good pass. Should he lose the ball, your decision to pass to him is as much to blame as his shortcomings.

Being a good *distributor*—or passer—involves knowing your teammates. Mine have included Gerd Mueller and Branko Segota, two exceptional strikers. Even so, I had to treat them quite differently.

Gerd was stocky and slow but quite powerful. Branko is lightning quick but not as strong. With Branko, it's often a good idea to play the ball into space where he can use his speed and quickness to beat his marker to the ball before accelerating past any remaining defenders.

The same pass, no matter how well executed, would be wasted if a Gerd Mueller were the intended receiver. With Gerd, it was best to play the ball to his feet where he could shield it and either play a complementary pass for a teammate moving goalward or pivot to take his defender on. The same pass to Branko would rarely work. He would most likely be out-muscled by a bigger, stronger defender.

In your case, I'm sure you have some teammates who are fast and others who are slow. Some are strong; some aren't. Some are right footed, and others are lefties. A few may be able to bring the most difficult service under control instantly, while others miss the easiest situations. You may have all the touches in the world in your bag of tricks, but until your judgment equals your technical skill, you will not be a good passer.

## READING THE GAME

Of course, knowing your rivals is also a factor. The smart player is aware of what weaknesses he can exploit in the opposing defense. Is their back line *flat?* That is, are their players on the same plane? If so, a *through ball* into the space behind them for a teammate of yours to run into is in order. If they're small, perhaps a high cross into the penalty area will cause them the most concern. If they mark loosely, play passes to your teammates' feet.

These decisions are based on what is known as *reading the game*. It is your ability to recognize, analyze and then capitalize on what's most appropriate in a given situation.

Left: Passing is one of soccer's most important skills, as shown here by Ray Hudson, the NASL's third all-time assist leader. (Gail Traendly)

## SPEED AND SIMPLICITY

Another significant ability is the skill of passing on the first touch. There are times when the other team's defense is scrambling, caught out of position. If you must trap the ball first before being able to pass it, you will inadvertently give your opponents time to recover. Being able to pass the ball while you're on the move, on the first touch, is an asset.

Another attribute of a good passer is the ability and inclination to play simply. There will be occasions when a spectacular 40-yard pass will set one of your teammates free for a shot on goal. But over the course of an entire match, that situation may present itself just a few times, if at all.

Most of the game is likely to involve short passes to nearby players. To pick the right option and execute it properly you need to master the ball so you can kick it quickly without looking at it.

## PUSH PASS

The most common pass you'll need happens to be the easiest, most effective, and simplest to control. It's also safe and accurate.

As the name suggests, the ball is *pushed* to a teammate. You use the flat, inside part of your shoe against the center of the ball. As with nearly all soccer touches, point your supporting foot at your target. It should be parallel to the motion of the ball and a few inches from the ball.

Your kicking leg should swing like a pendulum, with your knee bent and slightly ahead of your foot. Doing this angles your foot downward. This helps your pass to roll, making it easier for the receiver to trap. Also, it increases your ability to strike the ball correctly when making a first-touch pass, should the ball take a bad hop just as you're kicking it.

A little-regarded but important factor is to lean forward and over the ball. This is just one more step toward dispatching casualness and replacing it with solid technique and urgency.

**Cheating** — A lot of you beginners may lose some balance when first attempting the push pass. This is natural. What is equally common is for you to "cheat" by bringing your foot across your body as you hit the ball.

It is quite possible to do this and still make an accurate pass when the ball is rolling smoothly and your receiver is nearby. However, when you get in games, with the ball skipping, teammates and opponents moving, and time of the essence, improper technique will become apparent. Be sure that all of your push passes, no matter how easy they may seem, find your foot square to your target. Swing that foot straight back and straight forward.

**Proper Feel**—To get the proper feel for the motion, stand with your supporting foot pointed at your target. Take your kicking foot and place it at a 90° angle to your supporting foot. Its heel meets the inside center of your planted shoe.

Bring your kicking foot six inches away from your supporting leg while bending the

**PUSH PASS**

1) Use the inside of your shoe.

2) Keep your knee bent so your foot strikes the center of the ball.

3) Follow-through at your target. (Jim Frank)

knee. The kicking foot is now four to six inches off the ground. With your knee slightly in front of the foot, you are now in the proper alignment to strike the push pass.

### OUTSIDE-OF-THE-FOOT PUSH PASS

When time and space are limited, you may want to play the ball back to the person who sent it to you, assuming that person is running alongside you. In this case, the outside of your shoe comes into play. As with the conventional push pass, a flat surface is best for accuracy. Because your knee cannot bend backward, little power is generated. Therefore, this pass is effective only over very short distances, rarely more than 10 to 15 yards.

The foot closer to the incoming ball is used. This is one of the very few times in soccer in which your supporting foot does not point at the receiver. Because you kick the ball while moving, it is impractical to turn your opposite foot in a direction other than the one in which you are running.

Your kicking foot will pass over the supporting foot on its "backswing," which is actually a sideswing. Once again, strike the center of the ball with the flat portion of your shoe before following through at your target.

### BACK-HEEL PASS

This is another effective on-the-run pass. Let's say you're dribbling toward the other team's goal and several defenders are in good position to block your path. There are no teammates in front or to your side who are open for a pass.

**BACK-HEEL PUSH PASS**
Notice how the foot is parallel to the ground on impact. The heel strikes the center of the ball. (Dan Herbst)

In this case, chances are that someone behind you may be unmarked. To deliver the ball as quickly as possible to him, merely step over it and move your heel backward. Your heel should strike the center of the ball. You want your kicking foot to be parallel to the ground as it meets the ball.

The supporting foot should be next to the ball. If it's either in front of or behind the ball, you'll hit the ball on the upswing or downswing. The ball will then bounce, making it much tougher for your teammate to control.

Incidentally, don't spend excessive time perfecting this pass. It's used only occasionally. Your time is best spent by concentrating on perfecting the push pass, which is the key service in every passer's game.

## INSTEP PASS

So far, all of the passes discussed are used when the receiver is nearby and accuracy is the key ingredient. However, there will be times when you have a wide-open teammate who is far away. In this case, you must kick the ball with power. The precision required in a push pass isn't necessary here, although you can't hit the ball aimlessly.

The most common long pass involves using your instep — the arched upper surface of your foot, a few inches above your toes.

Generally speaking, the ball and your intended receiver will be moving. It is *vital* that you redouble your concentration on striking the ball cleanly. In other words, don't try to "kill" it. Be certain you swing your foot at a controllable speed. Be sure that the *sweet spot,* or center, of the ball is met by the sweet spot of your shoes — the laces.

**INSTEP PASS**
Use this for long passes. Notice how Cosmos star defender Andranik Eskandarian has his supporting foot pointed at his target. (Milton Crossen)

As you approach the ball, your knee should be ahead of your kicking foot. Your supporting foot should be next to the ball and pointing at your target.

This technique is the same as the instep drive shot, with one exception. If you wish to add height to your kick — at the expense of power — to loft it over a defender, lean backward. This forces the toes of your kicking foot to scoop under the ball, making it rise.

Whether you hit the ball low and hard, or high, follow through by pointing your kicking foot at your target. Because the ball can take unpredictable hops, keep your eye on it until your foot is following through.

On impact try to have your hips and shoulders square to the ball. This will prevent your kicking foot from moving across the ball and curving the ball off-target.

## OUTSIDE-OF-THE-FOOT-PASS

When you've reached an advanced level of proficiency, you may be able to use the outside of your foot for long passes. Franz Beckenbauer, the great ex-Cosmo and West German star, used this technique to swerve the ball around an opponent and onto a teammate's foot.

Having played against Franz in several NASL matches, I can testify how effective this pass can be. However, it is also extraordinarily difficult. Only advanced players should attempt it.

Even so, here's how to do it: The key is to be able to use a very small portion of the outside of your shoe to meet a very small portion of the ball. The part of the shoe just behind the small toe contacts the outside panel of the ball closest to your supporting foot.

Your kicking foot moves between the supporting foot and the ball in an inside-out motion. Your toes are pointed slightly downward. Your foot is behind the ball as it approaches. Your foot then moves circularly—clockwise for a right-footed kick, counterclockwise when using your left foot. Follow-through has your foot moving away from your body. This helps impart spin on the ball.

Sound complicated? It is. And it's a lot tougher when the ball is moving, the field is not level and a marker is on you. As I said, leave this pass to the experts.

## CHIP PASS

Another advanced pass is the chip. This occurs when there is a defender between you and your receiver. If your teammate has some space and time to control the ball as it arrives, you may wish to loft a pass over the defender.

You can do this by pointing your toes downward and stabbing the ball of your kicking foot into the ground. Little or no follow-through is necessary. Your supporting foot points at the ball and your entire body is square to it. The instep strikes the bottom of the ball.

**CHIP PASS**
1) To chip the ball, point the toes of your kicking foot directly ahead.

2) Jab that foot into the underside of the ball.

3) Minimize follow-through so the ball pops up. (Jim Frank)

As in golf's chip shot, the chip pass requires a delicate touch and a lot of accuracy. Done incorrectly, your pass will either fly over your teammate's head or strike the defender. Either way, you'll probably lose the ball.

Learning how to hit the ball just hard enough to get it over the defender, yet soft enough to be controlled by your receiver, takes plenty of practice. You'll find that it's easiest to chip a ball that is rolling toward you, a bit trickier to pass one that is still, and almost impossible to loft one that is rolling away from you.

## THROW-INS

There is only one type of pass in which an *outfield* player—a non-goalie—may use his hands: the *throw-in*. It's important to consider the throw-in a form of passing. Too often the thrower neglects the factors that make a pass successful, especially *consideration,* as discussed earlier.

Similarly, receivers of throw-ins must ease the thrower's task by giving themselves space. If they're too close to the thrower, all they do is make the defender's job easier and increase the likelihood of an illegal toss.

Receivers should be far enough away from the sideline so they can move toward the ball as it's thrown. Of course, not everyone makes a similar run. Others may criss-cross or move toward space downfield. A variety of off-the-ball movement gives the thrower many options from which to select the best. Several throw-in plays are covered later in this book.

**Rules**—According to the laws of the game, the ball must be propelled equally with both hands, which must travel behind your head so follow-through is a natural motion. You can't drop the ball onto the field. It must be thrown.

At least a part of each foot must remain in contact with the ground until your entire motion is complete. You must throw the ball in the direction you're facing. You must release the ball from the approximate spot where the ball left the playing area.

In addition, you may not re-enter the field until your motion is completed. In most leagues, this is interpreted that at least a part of each foot must be behind or on the line. However, some North American leagues require that all parts of both feet remain behind the entire line.

Either way, you'll get more power, and distance, by holding the ball correctly and using all of your upper-body strength by arching your back.

Your fingers grip the sides of the ball with your thumbs behind and to its bottom. Lean back from your waist to get added thrust if great distance is desired.

To avoid an illegal throw, it's a good habit to touch the ball to the back of your neck before beginning your forward motion.

Should your throw violate any of these regulations, the other team will be awarded a throw-in.

**THROW-IN**
Consider the throw-in a pass!

**ILLEGAL THROW-IN**
If your foot leaves the ground, your throw is illegal and the other team will
be awarded a throw-in from that spot. (Jim Frank)

## PASSING STRATEGIES

Just as there are different techniques used to propel a ball, so, too, are there categories and strategies of passes. Soccer lingo has plenty of colorful phrases to describe these different types of passes. There are *through balls, killer passes* and *wall passes*. There are even *square passes*. Perhaps the pass requiring the greatest intelligence of all is known as the *dummy*.

**Wall Pass**—In basketball, the most basic pass is called the *give-and-go*. Soccer's equivalent involves a first-touch return pass to the player who originally played it.

As the accompanying photo sequence illustrates, the man in possession is tightly marked. Rather than attempting to dribble past his defender, he passes the ball. As soon as it leaves his foot, he sprints around the outside of his man. The receiver moves toward the incoming ball and, using the push pass—with either the inside or the outside of his foot, whichever is closer to the ball—places it into space for the original passer to run to.

By running around the far side of his man, the eventual receiver has a better angle to accept the ball and has forced his marker to turn away from it. This gives him an important extra half-step that can prove invaluable.

When making the wall pass back to your teammate, concentrate on striking the ball so that your service is easy to control. You'll need just a very short leg swing because the ball already has plenty of pace. Be sure to hit the middle of the ball with the widest part of your foot.

Avoid the common mistake of being stiff. Keep both knees slightly bent.

**WALL PASS**
1) When struck in *front* of the receiver, a wall pass is an effective way to advance upfield. (Jim Frank)

2) Here, the receiver gets the ball as the passer runs upfield.

3) The original passer gets the ball back from the receiver and is now in front of his marker.

**Through Ball** — Most passes are simple touches designed to maintain possession. The idea is to put your team in a better position to advance the ball. However, there are times when a pass must go through or over several opponents.

A through ball is, as the name implies, one that is received by an attacker behind defenders between him and the passer. A good through pass puts those opponents out of position.

**Killer Pass** — This goes to a receiver who has timed his movements so he is onside when the ball is played forward. He gains possession behind all of the defenders except, perhaps, the goalie. This term is used to refer to a pass that leads directly to a great scoring opportunity.

**Square Pass** — Before you can play a through ball, a *square pass* is often needed. This is a pass that travels parallel to the goal line. It is usually made to a teammate who has a better angle at which to play the ball forward. See the accompanying drawings.

Later in this chapter you'll find some helpful exercises to teach and learn both the technical and tactical skills involved.

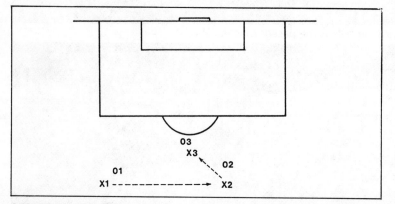

**SQUARE PASS #1**
Players X1 and X2 are marked. Their teammate, X3, is not. To get the ball to X3, X1 would have to chip the ball over defender O2, a tricky proposition at best. Instead, he makes a square pass to X2, who has an easy angle to pass to X3.

**Back Pass** — The greatest difference between professional or collegiate soccer and the youth game is the direction of most of our passes. Among the pros and in college, we utilize both skill and patience. We maintain possession of the ball whenever possible.

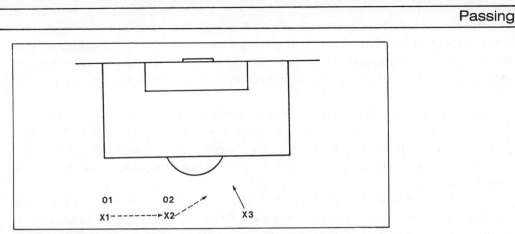

**SQUARE PASS #2**
In this situation, X2 again has a better angle to attempt a through pass. The square pass from X1 initiates a forward movement. It is important for players to think a couple of passes ahead, as X1 illustrates here.

This means that if no one in front of the ball is in a good position to receive a pass, we'll play the ball *backward* to a supporting teammate. Chances are that he'll have a better angle to play the ball upfield, a better range of vision to see where open players are located, and he'll be unmarked.

In general, the backward pass, or *back pass,* is used by a player near a sideline. If he's well marked, and outnumbered, then his team has a numerical advantage at some other point on the field. Most likely, it's on the opposite side.

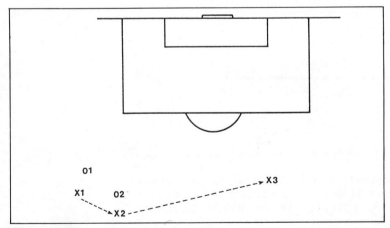

**BACK PASS**
Here, X1 passes back to X2 so he can then pass to X3. Generally, this is easier than X1 passing directly to X3.

To get the ball there, you should start playing it backward. The supporting player then passes square or diagonally forward — or dribbles in either of those directions. On occasion, the supporting player may have an angle that makes a through wall pass the ideal choice.

Keep in mind that the supporting player should not be too close to the player in possession. If he is, he'll have a defender on him as soon as he gets the back pass. If he's too far away, he allows another opponent the chance to cut between him and the ball.

In general, the supporting player should be at a 45° angle and about 10 yards from the man in possession.

In youth soccer, you won't see many back passes. In fact, it's rare until athletes reach their mid-teens. I suggest that you coaches not be dismayed with your charges even if they continually play the ball forward when all their open teammates are to their sides or behind them. Going forward is a matter of instinct. It takes years of experience, and a lot of skill, to make the right decision consistently.

**Dummy**—Speaking of maneuvers that require vision, here's a pass that demands no physical soccer skill to execute, yet only the greatest of passers can make it. And, if it's so ingenious, why the seemingly derogatory name? Puzzled?

Actually, the title derives from the term *selling an opponent the dummy*. The dummy can be used anywhere on the field although it's not a very good idea in front of your own goal. It is especially effective in and around the other team's penalty area. There, defenders are so concerned with their opponents and the ball that they're very vulnerable to this unpredictable deception.

A well-acted dummy will "freeze" them just long enough for you to be effective.

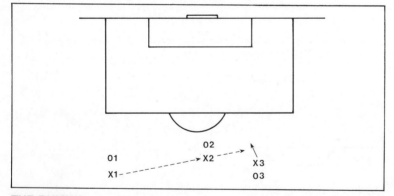

**THE DUMMY**
The striker X2 is tightly marked. He knows that he has little or no time in which to receive a pass from X1, turn, and get the ball to X3. In fact, by the time he did all of that, X3's marker could recover and get into a good defending position.

Instead, X2 moves as if to play the ball. You can be sure that his marker will stay right with him. At the last instant, X2 lets the ball roll through his legs. His defender, fooled by X2's body motion, has forgotten about the ball. It arrives to present X3 with a great scoring opportunity.

## PASSING PRACTICE

You *must* be a good passer to play soccer at an advanced level. That skill has to result from many hours of practice. However, training need not be a burden. Lots of passing games are both constructive and fun. Best of all, you can play some of them alone.

**The Wall**—There's another form of *wall pass,* besides the one discussed earlier. This one doesn't occur in a game. It literally involves a wall. All you need is a building wall—preferably one without windows if you're a beginner—and a ball.

As a kid, I spent entire afternoons challenging myself to see if I could "beat" the wall. I'd try to strike 10 straight passes from a set distance that would hit a target on the wall. As I got better, I'd try to make 10 straight first-touch passes. Or do it with my weaker foot. Or alternate feet. Or use the inside and then the outside of the feet—whatever was an appropriate challenge.

The great thing about a wall is that it never "lies" or misses. If the ball doesn't arrive directly back to your feet, your initial pass was inadequate. You will now receive "passes," some of which may take bad bounces. This forces you to make good distributions, just as in a match.

## TWO-PLAYER DRILLS AND GAMES

To really sharpen passing skills, you need a friend. If your entire team is present, you can do these exercises in pairs.

**Accuracy Drill**—The simplest one has you and your partner standing from 5 to 20 yards apart, depending on your skill level. The person without the ball stands with his legs a bit wider than shoulder width. The player with the ball tries to pass it through his teammate's legs. Take turns passing, with the first one to complete five successful passes declared the winner.

**Jogging Drill**—A good drill to develop passing skill and fitness is to pass the ball back and forth as you jog around the field. There are several variations on this, including using a third player.

Other variations include one man running backward and the other forward, which is good for balance and touch. Or, if you're all moving in the same direction, follow your pass by running around and behind the receiver. This teaches you to stay in the play even after you've released the ball. After the pass, advance into a good attacking position so you're available to receive the ball again.

## TEAM PASSING DRILLS AND GAMES

These exercises simulate the passing requirements of game situations. They offer the extra benefit of letting you do them over and over until the strategies and combinations become automatic.

**Circle Drill** — This is perhaps the best and most commonly used team practice. A group of players forms a circle with one or two defenders in the middle. Players on the outside must pass the ball to each other, while those in the middle try to intercept it.

There are two ways to play. One is *cutthroat.* When the ball is picked off by a center player or players, he or they exchange places with the same number of outside players. In other words, if there were two men in the middle, both the outside man who made the errant pass and his intended receiver would become defenders. The two defenders now move to the outside of the circle.

Another variation is to play games of 10 points. Use two or three center players and five to eight outside men. (The ratio of outside to center players varies and should become smaller as skill level improves.) Attackers are awarded a point whenever they make a predesignated number of consecutive successful passes. They get two points for any penetrating pass — when they play the ball through the defense to a teammate on the opposite side. As for the defense, they get a point whenever a pass breaks the plane of the circle or when they touch the ball.

Try to maintain a competitive balance. If the offense keeps winning, either alter the manpower ratio or require a greater number of passes to be completed before recording a score. Conversely, if the defense keeps prevailing, relax the requirement or enhance the attacker/defender ratio.

If your team is quite advanced, try the circle drill with everyone required to pass the ball on the first touch.

**Square Drill** — To sharpen one-touch distribution, you can also use a square and four players, as shown in the accompanying drawing. Player A has the ball and has B and C as potential targets. Player X is the defender.

This drill teaches several important lessons: First, players off the ball must move to free themselves *before* the defense gets set. Second, the receiver must have good vision so he can anticipate which teammate is in the best position to receive his pass. Third and most important, the passing must be done quickly and while under defensive pressure in a confined area.

Advanced? Sure it is. But younger players can partake and benefit from it, too. Simply adjust the size of the practice square. For example, 10x10 yards is good for high-school players, and 20x20 yards is fine for less-skilled athletes.

Either way, the defender will get plenty of exercise. Don't keep him in there for over a minute, if that long. For this drill to be beneficial, the defender must exert maximum pressure on the attackers. Nobody, present company included, can be expected to sprint, change direction and sprint again for more than 60 seconds.

**Other Drills**—There are plenty of simple ones. After the two-man-passing-back-and-forth series, have two lines of players facing each other. Have the front men in each group 10 to 20 yards apart.

The player at the front of the first line passes to his counterpart in line two. After passing, he runs to the back of the opposite line. The receiver traps the ball and repeats the procedure by passing to a different lead man.

As skills improve, passes should be made on the first touch, or with the weaker foot only.

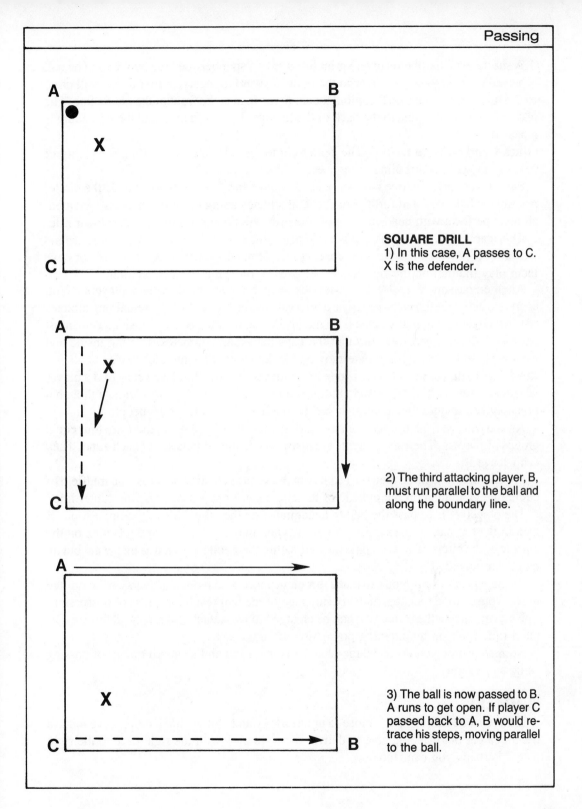

**SQUARE DRILL**
1) In this case, A passes to C. X is the defender.

2) The third attacking player, B, must run parallel to the ball and along the boundary line.

3) The ball is now passed to B. A runs to get open. If player C passed back to A, B would retrace his steps, moving parallel to the ball.

A similar drill has the receiver sprint forward to a spot between the two lines. The ball is played to him by the passer, who then runs forward to receive a first-touch wall pass. He, in turn, passes, also on the initial touch, to the man at the front of the facing line. The player in the middle runs to the back of the line that he was facing, and the procedure is repeated.

**Other Center-Circle Drills**—The center circle provides an ideal setting for plenty of passing, as well as dribbling, exercises.

Pair players off with one ball per pair. On command, they must jog inside the circle, passing the ball back and forth. With several athletes doing the same in a confined area, all must perform with heads up. If not, the drill will soon resemble a bumper-car ride.

This teaches players to pass, move to space and be aware of what is happening around the ball. As players improve, you coaches can demand specific types of passes or have them play the ball on the first touch. Also work on using the weaker foot.

Another passing exercise that uses the center circle involves two players. With everyone else standing at 5- to 10-yard intervals on the circle, the two remaining athletes run around their teammates. One is on the inside and the other on the outside. They must pass the ball back and forth through the gaps between teammates. Use the inside and outside of both feet and alternate moving clockwise and counterclockwise.

**Inside-Outside Game** — Here is one game that is so much fun I've yet to find a player who doesn't enjoy it. When I was a kid, we called it the *Inside-Outside Game,* although it probably has many other names. It can be played with 8, 12 or 16 people.

As you can see from the accompanying drawing using 12 players, there are four equal groups of players. Their movements are restricted by the boundaries of each zone. They can't leave it.

For example, the three men on Team A in the semicircle may not cross the midfield or circle line. The men on the outside of the circle can't enter it or cross the center line.

The objective is to pass the ball to a teammate on the other side of the opposition. B men in the top half of the circle score only when they get the ball to the B men on the outside of the circle. They can pass the ball within their zone as much as they want but no points are awarded.

As players gain skill, you can make this game more demanding. Players can be limited to two consecutive touches, and any stoppage of the ball results in a loss of possession. The players inside the semicircle can be changed to two attackers and one defender. Or, put a time limit on maintaining possession within a zone.

No matter how you do it, Inside-Outside is great fun and a superb trainer of passing skills and vision.

## SUMMARY

If there's one subject that's close to my heart — and feet — it's passing. I've made a decent career out of being able to deliver the right pass with the right pace to the right place. Perhaps you can, too.

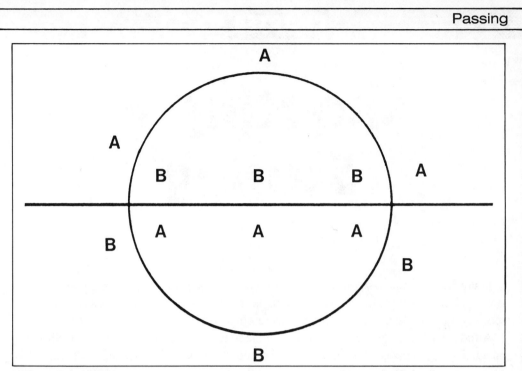

**INSIDE-OUTSIDE GAME**
Here's a way to set up 12 players for this fun game, as described on page 84.

It *does* take practice. I've given you a few ideas for training activities, but there are many more. Don't be limited by the conventional. Use your imagination.

Nobody has greater imagination than youngsters. You developing players should feel free to invent games. If they're good, send me the details. I can use the practice, too!

The most important thing, just as with all forms of ball control, is repetition of proper technique. I can't emphasize enough how important it is to have a sense of urgency behind every pass, yet always strive for pinpoint accuracy. Develop good technique. Concentrate fully on delivering every pass properly, no matter how simple.

A great passer makes the ball do the work for him. That's why exceptional distributors of the ball, like Beckenbauer, can play at the highest levels of soccer at an age when others have long since been forced into retirement.

To me, there is no greater satisfaction than making an outstanding pass that sets up a match-winning goal. When that happens, it's the result of hours spent with a wall or a few teammates.

But even if that moment never came, I'd still have enjoyed my training sessions. The games listed here have a dual purpose — they build skill and are fun. That's what soccer is all about.

# CHAPTER SIX

# Shooting & Scoring

I may be a veteran now, but I can still remember what it was like as a kid playing in the streets of Newcastle. Practically every game included some form of shooting and goal scoring. Left to our own devices, we were constantly taking shots at goal.

Although we had no way of knowing it at the time, our instincts were correct. Shooting on goal — also called *finishing* — is the most important, most difficult and most enjoyable aspect of the game.

On almost any good team, from youth leagues to the pros, the most significant single player is the *striker,* also known as the center-forward. His job demands the most of everything, from technique to temperament. If his task isn't carried out correctly, all the good defense, build-up and hard work of his teammates will be rendered meaningless.

To be an outstanding goal scorer, you need more than just skill. Certainly, the technical ability to shoot accurately, quickly and with power in a confined area is rare. There are some occasions when the striker has lots of time and space, and others where everything must be done in a split second. Knowing just how much time is available and the best type of shot to use comes only through experience.and composure.

Entire games, and World Cups too, have been decided by the superiority of one player. For example, in 1982, Brazil dazzled hundreds of millions of fans with grace and skill. But Italy, with a hot Paolo Rossi, won the Cup.

It's not much different from Saturday-morning games in the park. Certainly, the skill level isn't the same, but the attributes that can make you a good goal scorer are.

As discussed in this chapter, there is a wide variety of shots. Each has a special attribute in its favor, but only for a specific situation. As a striker, you'll need to decide *before the ball arrives* which card to pick from soccer's deck. This is what makes finishing such an art.

Right: Here's Ray against arch-rival Tampa Bay, showing the form that has produced 44 NASL goals. (Jon Van Woerden)

## STRIKER CHARACTERISTICS

Throughout my career I've played with and against some great strikers. Included on the list is Gerd Mueller. *Der Bomber* won an unprecedented seven scoring titles in the *Bundesliga,* the West German first division. In addition, he scored 68 goals in 62 international matches—including the winner in the 1974 World Cup Final against Holland. And he holds the single-season Striker scoring record, a feat I was happy to "assist" him in achieving.

Getting to play with and observe Mueller firsthand has been a thrill and revelation for me. He isn't very fast. He's certainly short. And his dribbling skills are conventional. Yet, this barrel-shaped man is probably the greatest European goal scorer of our time. How could that be?

For one thing, Mueller was mentally fast. He couldn't beat all defenders in a footrace, but through incredible anticipation and knowledge, he always had a one-step headstart on his rival. All Gerd needed was a first touch of the ball. In addition, he had a keen awareness of the geometry of the penalty area. Without having to look up, he knew exactly where he was relative to the goal by checking field markings.

Another vital Mueller asset was confidence. Even if he was having an off-day—in fact, a terrible game—he was always certain that he would find a way to score. *All* great strikers enjoy the responsibility that comes with their position. They thrive on pressure rather than succumb to it. It's been said that superior finishers need a touch of arrogance in their personality. Though there were many exceptional finishers who were modest about their deeds—including my teammate Brian Kidd—unbridled self-belief is necessary. After all, even the best players experience much more frustration than success.

It's a fact that a baseball hitter is a hero even if he fails seven times out of 10. For a striker, the percentage is worse.

**A Word To Coaches**—What do these qualities have to do with an eight-year-old player? Plenty. It's important for you youth coaches to truly appreciate just how difficult scoring is.

It's imperative that you always encourage your kids to take a shot at goal. Even if a player misses the ball completely, applaud him for the attempt. Remember, he had to do a lot of things right just to earn the opportunity. Let him know that you appreciate what it took for him to be in a goal-scoring position instead of deriding him for failing to finish.

Because confidence is a vital a part of the goal scorer's game, never do anything to hinder his mental outlook.

Keep in mind that finishers can only be developed through years of hard work and practice. Virtually every training session should include some form of shooting. You can incorporate it into a regular game, but be sure to feature it at every practice. Not only will this be more fun for your players, but it will also help them improve the most decisive skill in the game.

In this chapter I discuss various training games and drills utilized to sharpen finishing skills. First, let's examine the types of shots most commonly used.

## INSTEP DRIVE

The instep drive is to a goal scorer what a paintbrush is to an artist. There are several important shots, but the instep drive is the one you *must* master if you're to become a consistent scorer, regardless of your age. The beauty of this shot is that, when made correctly, it is both powerful and accurate.

Essentially, it has the same technique that so-called soccer-style place kickers use to make field goals and extra points in American football. There is one minor exception. The soccer player must propel the ball with power, but keep the ball below the eight-foot crossbar of the goal. That's much more difficult than kicking a ball *over* a target.

To shoot the instep drive, you approach the ball from a 45° angle. To shoot with your right foot, start to the left of and behind where you will kick the ball. Thus, you're moving toward the right corner flag, not toward your target, the goal.

As you approach the ball, your supporting foot plants alongside it. Your foot should point at the goal and be a few inches to the left of the ball.

While you're planting your supporting foot, the rest of your frame—from shoulders through your hips—remains directed toward the corner flag. As you bring your kicking foot backward, that knee is over the ball and the toes of that foot point downward.

It's now time to bring your foot forward to meet the ball. As your downswing proceeds, your hips and shoulders will automatically pivot to face the direction pointed to by your supporting foot. Thus, if your supporting leg is properly aligned, your body will be square to the goal as you strike the ball.

**INSTEP DRIVE**
To keep your shots low on the instep drive, get the knee of your kicking foot over the ball. Keep your toes down for as long as possible on the follow-through. (Dan Herbst)

As foot meets ball, your toes remain pointed toward the turf. They are a few inches farther from your supporting foot than is the heel of your kicking foot. Because you are angling your foot, the instep will hit the ball.

As you follow through, keep your toes down and move your leg directly ahead so it moves in the direction you're aiming toward.

**What To Avoid**—Here are some common mistakes to avoid: First, do not open your upper body prematurely. A lot of players, including some pros, mishit the instep drive because of this. Instead of a straight leg swing, they come across the ball and hit it with the inside of their shoe. This reduces accuracy *and* power. You want to use your knee as a fulcrum, which is possible only if your upper body is properly aligned. This means that your toes face down and your knee is over the ball as you address it.

Second, don't overhit your shot. In most match situations, the ball will be rolling. If you execute proper technique and strike the ball cleanly, you'll get more than enough pace on your shot. Those who try to "kill" the ball find that the shot either sails harmlessly over the crossbar or trickles off the side of their foot.

Third, check the position of your kicking foot. Keep those toes down and slightly inward.

Proper foot position when striking the instep drive. (Dan Herbst)

To get the feel for that position, try the following: Place the ball on the ground and stand next to it. With your supporting foot aimed at your target and your upper body facing the corner flag, reach back with your right hand and grasp the kicking foot. Pull your heel backward so that it nearly touches your rear end. Let go of the foot and let it swing forward naturally.

Once you try it, you'll discover a "funny" thing happens. Without having swung your leg fast, and with no body momentum at all, you can still hit the shot with authority. This indicates that proper technique, *not* a hard leg swing or fast approach, generates most of the power of the instep drive.

**More Power and Accuracy**—Both can be improved by transferring body weight from the supporting foot to the kicking foot as you strike the ball. Be on the toes of the supporting foot as you strike the ball. Land on the kicking foot after following through. This keeps your toes pointed downward to keep the shot low and powerful.

If you still find that many of your shots are too high, concentrate on getting your knee and shoulders over the ball as you address it. The position of your toes—as well as leaning forward or backward—help determine the shot's altitude.

Notice how the left heel rises a bit on the follow-through of the instep drive.

## PUSH-PASS SHOT

A surprising number of goals—especially in indoor soccer—are scored from short distances on deflections and by redirecting the ball. The closer you are to the goalie, the more important accuracy is than power. A shot from 10 yards need not move fast if it's directed just inside the goalpost. But even at the higher levels of soccer, the tendency to overhit a shot—sacrificing accuracy for power—is the main cause of squandered scoring chances.

One way of guarding against this is to literally *pass* the ball into the net. By using the flat, inside portion of your shoe, you use maximum foot surface in the finish. Fine accuracy results.

As the ball approaches, you point that supporting foot at your target. Turn your kicking foot sideways so the inside part of your shoe is parallel to the target. Bring that leg straight back and straight forward in a sweeping motion. By bending your knee and keeping it slightly ahead of your kicking foot, you can strike the middle of the ball to keep the shot on the ground. That's the toughest of all places for a goalkeeper to make a clean save.

As always, follow through directly at your target.

**PUSH-PASS SHOT**
When you're close to the goal, accuracy is important, not power. To score, use the inside of your foot to push pass the ball into the net. (Jim Frank)

## TOE POKE

Let's say you're one-on-one with the goalie, who is advancing rapidly toward you. You have no time to wind up for a shot because he may throw his body across your path as your foot meets the ball. What to do?

In this situation, the toe poke is most appropriate. Jab the front of your shoe into the middle of the ball. Why the ball's center? Because if you hit under the ball, it will fly upward, where the goalie can more readily deflect it with his hand. By hitting the middle of the ball, or just above it, you keep the shot as low as possible.

The toe poke certainly looks awkward and ungainly but, when used in the right situation, it can be most effective.

**TOE POKE**
Here's the foot position for the toe poke, an ungainly, but effective shot when used correctly. (Jim Frank)

## VOLLEY

Sometimes the ball arrives not at your feet, but in midair. And on occasion, especially in the penalty area, you may not have enough time and space in which to trap the ball before shooting it. In this case, a first-touch shot is necessary.

Known as the *volley,* it is an extremely effective weapon that can catch the goalie offguard. However, it is also one of the toughest shots to control. Even in the pros, a great percentage of volleys fly well above the target. An ex-teammate of mine, Marinho, was dubbed *Mezzanineho* by a sharp-witted broadcaster because of his habit for sending shots toward the sky.

The "rules" on keeping all shots low apply to the volley, too: Get your knee above the ball; keep your toes pointed downward from backswing to the conclusion of your follow-through; watch the ball onto your foot; and, if possible, land on your kicking foot.

Because the ball will be moving quickly, you'll have no trouble hitting it hard if the sweet spot of your instep strikes the sweet spot (center) of the ball.

When aiming the ball back in the direction from which it came, get your entire frame square to the goal. Bend your kicking leg from the knee. In some cases, you'll need to jump so your kicking foot can be extended as it hits the ball. Use a limited follow-through to help keep your shot under control.

**VOLLEY**
To keep the ball from flying over the crossbar, point your toes downward. Get that knee over the ball, and make sure you strike the ball with your supporting foot next to it, not behind it! (Jim Frank)

## HALF VOLLEY

The half volley is a first-touch shot in which you strike the ball just after it has left the ground. Recommended form is basically the same as with the volley, although you are rarely airborne. Concentrate on getting your kicking knee—and in turn your kicking foot—above and in front of the ball before impact.

## SIDE VOLLEY

Perhaps the toughest volley of all comes when you're asked to redirect a cross that comes from the sideline. Known as the *side volley,* it requires timing, coordination, concentration, agility and, obviously, plenty of practice.

The starting position finds your body perpendicular to the ball's line of flight. For example, if the cross travels from the right-corner flag, the body should be square to the right-corner flag. Use the foot that's closer to the incoming ball to kick it. In this case, the ball is arriving on your right side, so use your right foot.

As the cross arrives, your supporting foot pivots to point at your target. Move it counterclockwise for a right-footed shot and clockwise when shooting with your left foot.

**SIDE VOLLEY**
As with the other volley shots, it will have plenty of power if you just concentrate on hitting the center of the ball with your shoe laces. (Jim Frank)

95

Withdraw your kicking leg so that the bottom part of it—the segment below your knee—is parallel to the ground. Once again your knee is bent. This time, though, it is to the side of the ball. Your foot is behind the ball, as well. Your knee will lead your foot into action. Keep your toes an inch or two closer to the ground than your heel.

To produce a line-drive shot, move your foot forward so that it hits the center of the ball and is parallel to the turf throughout the forward swing.

To shoot downward, a most difficult proposition, begin with your foot above the ball's line of flight. Swing your leg slightly toward the ground. Your foot should hit just above the ball's center before it follows through toward the turf. Either way, your shoulders and hips must rotate as your leg moves forward. Both should be square to your target on impact and during the entire follow-through.

## OUTSIDE-OF-THE-FOOT SHOT

When deception is advantageous, such as a one-on-one confrontation in which you're a modest distance from the goalie, use the outside of your shoe to shoot. Just as with the outside-of-the-foot pass, it's a touch that only advanced players should attempt.

The technique is basically the same. When shooting with your right foot, the outside of that shoe strikes the far edge of the ball's left side. The impact area of your foot is just outside and behind your small toe.

Your foot swings behind the ball and follows through in a circular motion. Keep those toes down.

If done properly, a screwball-like effect results. This effectively widens the goal. When using your right foot, the ball will swerve from left to right. Therefore, if you aim to the goalie's right—your left—the ball should travel around his outstretched arms before curling into the net.

To impart spin and keep your shot low, strike the ball with the outside of your shoe. (Jim Frank)

## BANANA SHOT

Another way to get the shot to curve is to use the inside of your shoe against the far side of the ball. This time the ball will curve inward—for example to your left when you've shot with your right foot.

This technique is quite similar to the instep drive with the following exceptions: First, use the inside of your shoe with your toes pointed, but slightly downward. Second, come across the back of the ball and hit its far side. Third, follow through in a counterclockwise direction for a right-footed shot, or clockwise when using your left foot. This will cause your foot to come across the ball to impart spin. Fourth, lean your body away from the ball as you kick it.

In this case, aim the ball outside of the goalpost that's on the same side as your kicking foot. You should try to kick the ball with the foot opposite the near post. In other words, if you're to the left of the goal, use your right foot and aim to the right of the net. This will increase your angle.

When executing the banana shot, lean slightly backward and do not impart maximum power. This will make the ball float above the plane of the crossbar as it passes the goalie—who has come off the goal line to narrow your shooting angle—yet dip under the eight-foot high barrier when it reaches the goal.

**BANANA SHOT**
The banana shot is especially effective because it *looks* like an instep drive is coming to the goalie. This is the only shot in which you don't follow-through toward your target. (Jim Frank)

## CHIP SHOT

Sometimes a goalie, in his rush to limit a shooter's angle, will come too far off goal line. By doing so, he exposes himself to a chip, or lofted, shot. It goes over his head and sails into the net.

To chip a ball, use the same procedure as the instep drive. However, instead of leaning forward and over the ball as you shoot, lean backward. This will prevent your knee from getting above the ball. You toes will scoop under the ball, allowing them to point upward as you follow through.

Developing the right touch isn't easy. Remember, it will be less difficult to loft a ball that is rolling toward you. As with the banana shot, don't hit the ball too hard. Otherwise, it will have too much pace to dip in time.

## HEADER

When heading for goal, hit the upper part of the ball to make the shot descend. You must time your leap precisely and, if possible, get your forehead higher than the ball.

To loft the ball over the goalie, lean backward. To loft and curve it, lean away from the ball. (Stan Green)

## BICYCLE KICK

The most spectacular shot is the bicycle, or *scissors,* kick. But in all my years of playing I have never had an occasion to use it in a match. In fact, I've seen it attempted only a few times. But when it does occur, as when Klaus Fischer scored a dramatic goal for West Germany to tie the 1982 World Cup semi-final match with France in overtime, it is a moment that no fan or player will ever forget. As for the rest of us, it sure is fun to try in practice. It is also used to clear the ball out of your defensive third in an emergency.

The bicycle shot occurs when your back is to the goal as the ball arrives in midair. You use your non-kicking foot to propel your body backward off the ground. With your upper body parallel to the turf, your kicking foot moves toward your head as you strike the ball with your instep. Your hands cushion your eventual fall.

A word of caution, when first attempting it. Find a soft surface on which to land. In addition, should you perform a bicycle kick in a match, be certain you are in the open. If your foot is near an opponent as you kick the ball, you will be called for dangerous play, giving the other team an indirect free kick.

Although I've never used it to shoot in a match, I *have* made bicycle kicks to clear the ball out of danger. (Bob East III)

## HYBRID SHOTS

Not all instep drives find the ball neatly angled 45° from your kicking foot. If the ball is directly in front of you, combine the techniques used for the half volley and the instep drive. Improvisation, as well as skill, is the hallmark of the exceptional finisher.

## SUMMARY

As you can see, a goal-scorer has a number of shots in his arsenal. Many are advanced shots—too advanced, in fact, for most of you younger athletes. For you, I suggest sticking to mastering basic shots—the instep drive, the push-pass shot and the header. Until you feel comfortable with those, leave the fancy stuff to older, more experienced players.

No matter what method you use in a particular match situation, there are some constants that apply. Above all, accuracy is the basic requirement of consistent finishing. Never hit the ball any harder than necessary to get the job done.

**Anti-Goalie Strategy**—Except for lofted shots in certain situations, balls struck along the turf will bring the best results. Low balls are not only the most difficult for a goalie to reach. They're also the toughest to catch. Many times they will be deflected by the goalie back into play, giving you or a teammate a second chance at goal, while the goalie is down and out of position to make another save.

Here's another way to challenge the goalie: If a ball is crossed from the side, aim your shot in the direction from which the pass came. Generally, the goalie will be moving across his goal in the direction the ball *was* going. By shooting the ball in the opposite direction—behind his motion—you make his momentum work against him. Furthermore, you will also have a greater surface of the ball to strike, increasing the chance of a powerful and accurate finish.

**Attitude**—Concentration and sound judgment are but two of several required mental attributes. You need composure and courage to ignore some defenders' efforts to distract and intimidate.

You must also be confident. If you mishit a shot, do two things: First, analyze what technical flaw caused the poor result. Second, assure yourself that the next time you are presented with the same opportunity you will succeed.

I've seen too many players allow a mistake to adversely affect subsequent efforts. Many will be afraid of repeating an error and will pass the ball instead of shooting. That's the ultimate soccer copout. As far as I'm concerned, not taking a shot for that reason is a greater sin than a mishit.

## PRACTICE DRILLS AND GAMES

One of the best games is also one of the simplest. All you need is a friend, a ball and a goal without a net. Have your buddy stand on one side of the goal and you on the other, each the same distance from it. Try 10 to 15 yards apart for beginners, 20 to 30 yards for advanced players.

Have a contest to determine who is the first to score 10 goals. As you improve, add the stipulation that the ball must cross the goal line while airborne to be considered a score. In addition, you must hit the ball by the first, second or third touch, depending on your skill level.

A lot of you might wonder what is to be gained by shooting at a 192-square foot target that isn't even manned by a goalie. Actually, in many ways this is preferable to using a goalie. Because many players will try to overpower the shot to beat a goalie—and strike most of their shots incorrectly—an open net forces you to concentrate on proper technique. As your technique is upgraded, *then* work on adding pace to your shot.

Believe it or not, this exercise is tiring. That's also good because, in a game, technique often falters when fatigue is a factor. If you can learn to shoot a ball correctly when tired in practice, you'll probably be a "last-minute hero" during key games.

**With Goalie**—If you want to use a goalie in your practice, consider the following drills: For beginning players, have yourself and your teammates form a line across the 18-yard line. Number yourselves and have your coach call out numbers at random. When your number is called, have a shot at goal.

As you get better, move the line back five yards. This time when it's your turn, push the ball slightly ahead and kick it as it's rolling.

The next step up the ladder of finishing skills is to form a straight line facing the goal, about 30 yards from it. The front player push passes the ball to a server who is just outside the penalty box. The server produces a first-touch wall pass that the shooter must also kick on the initial touch.

Once you reach a plateau where you can *consistently* shoot with accuracy and the required amount of pace in this situation, you're ready for a tougher exercise. This one involves five shots on the run, each after receiving a pass from a new angle.

Place a cone, or a similar object, at the top of the penalty arc, which is 22 yards from the goal line. You, the shooter, stand on the penalty spot with your back to the net. Four teammates, each with a ball, form a square inside the box.

Start by sprinting around the cone before receiving a pass from player number one. As soon as you've shot, pivot and sprint around the cone again before repeating the procedure with player number two. Repeat with players three and four. After your fourth shot, your coach, positioned next to the cone, tosses a ball over your head as you run around the cone. Strike it on the volley.

This drill is extremely difficult. Do not become discouraged if many of your shots are mishit.

**Game Simulation**—All of these drills and games are beneficial, challenging and fun. Yet none can take the place of match experience. Because we play only so many games, it's helpful to simulate game conditions during practice. One way to do this is with games of few players, known as *small-sided games,* for example three vs. three up to six vs. six. Use goalies and full-size goals. Scale down field dimensions in proportion to the number of players.

## FINISHING DRILL WITH GOALIE

This drill uses a goalie and a server. It forces the shooter to finish while striking a rolling ball. (Jim Frank)

You'll find that scoring chances, while plentiful, must be taken quickly, just as in a match. Because they come unpredictably, having to select the right variety of shot is an added component.

**Advice**—As good as the other exercises are, they all involve premeditated technique. None is quite as useful for developing all of the traits needed to become a good finisher as small-sided games. However, unless you've reached a level in which your technique is sound, you run the risk of developing bad habits if your practices are more advanced than your skill level.

Your best bet is to progress at a pace that suits your ability. Stay with the basic drills until you are good enough to benefit from the next level of practice. However, you need not be advanced to enjoy small-sided games. They're great for all players.

Finally, do not become discouraged, either by your physical limitations or by a lack of technical proficiency. If you're not big and powerful, don't despair or try to make up for that by swinging wildly at the ball.

For example, Cubillas had precious little power. But he was a devastating finisher because he was one of the cleanest strikers of the ball ever. His grace under pressure, coupled with uncanny accuracy, made him one of the best scorers in World Cup history.

As for any technical flaws you may have, don't be overly concerned. Plenty of practice and playing diminishes them. Many top goal scorers did not excel as youths.

Keep working on fundamentals and concentrate on making good contact. Marry the sweet spot of your foot with the sweet spot of the ball. Before you know it, you too will become more of a scoring threat.

Perhaps you will share the most glorious moment of all—when one of your shots flies by the goalie into the back of the net. Believe me, that split-second provides such an exhilarating feeling that all the hours of practice are instantly rendered worthwhile.

# CHAPTER SEVEN

# Defending

Developing a soft touch on the ball is vital to becoming an outstanding player. But it represents only half of the story because as often as not, the other team will have the ball. To be an outstanding player you must be as good a defender as you are an attacker.

Too often, the fundamental skills of defense are neglected. That's probably because defending *appears* to be easy. In fact, defending requires technique, knowledge and plenty of practice.

Look at it this way—every attack begins when your team wins the ball! And the sooner your team wins it back—as well as the closer to the other side's goal—the better.

## ONE EXAMPLE

When the Chicago Sting captured Soccer Bowl-81, their high-powered offense garnered headlines. That summer the Sting scored a league-leading 81 goals in 32 regular season games—2.5 scores per match. They were led by two of the NASL's top seven scorers—Granitza (19 goals/17 assists) and Arno Steffenhagen (17/10). Overlooked in the shuffle was the work of American midfielder Rudy Glenn. Although he finished sixth in team scoring (7/0), Rudy was nearly as important to his team's attack as Granitza and Steffenhagen. And Glenn's role was predominately defensive.

It was his primary responsibility to be the defensive midfielder—the player who tried to get the ball from the opponent in possession. As soon as that was accomplished, Glenn would make a penetrating pass that started the Sting counterattack.

Often, Rudy would win the ball in the opponent's half of the field, giving Chicago rivals little time to make the transition from offense to defense. The result was a lot of goals by Granitza, Steffenhagen, Pato Margetic (8), Ingo Peter (8) and Charlie Fajkus (7).

In 1982, injuries forced the team to move Glenn to the backline. As a result, Chicago exerted less defensive pressure in the middle of the pitch. When they did regain possession, it was usually deep in their own territory, a position that made successful counterattacking difficult.

The often unheralded, but very important role performed by Chicago defensive midfielder Rudy Glenn (right) helped win a championship for the Sting. (Sting/Arthur Henning)

That year Ingo Peter didn't score a goal, Fajkus had only 2, Margetic slumped from 8 to 4 and Steffenhagen slid from 17 to 13. Only Granitza, with an extra score, enjoyed a comparable season as Chicago finished with a dismal 13-19 mark. I'm convinced that a big part of this was because they did not have an effective ball-winner in midfield.

There are some basic skills to defending—marking an opponent, jockeying him and tackling. This chapter also covers team defensive tactics such as supporting, making the transition from offense and defending against corner and free kicks.

## MARKING

You may think that covering an opponent would be easy, particularly when he doesn't have the ball. But at the highest levels of soccer, attackers off the ball are clever. They get into positions in which the defender cannot watch both them and the ball.

One of the most important factors in covering an opponent is deciding how close to be. If the ball is nearby and you're deep in your own territory, you should be within a few yards of him at all times—and between him and your goal. Otherwise, he can surprise you with a quick shot or a first-touch pass.

However, *marking* a man does not mean that you have to be "inside his shirt" all day. In fact, covering too close creates its own problems.

**Ball-Watching**—For example, when the ball is wide and your opponent is on the far side of the goal, you probably won't be able to watch both him and the ball. What he's hoping to do is lure you into concentrating exclusively on the ball—called *ball-watching*. When that happens, the crafty attacker will exploit your temporary lapse in concentration and run goalside of you. Before you realize what happened, he's free in your penalty area as the pass arrives.

You can avoid that. First, assume a stance that allows you improved all-around vision. Rather than facing him or the ball, open your stance so you can see both the ball and your opponent out of the opposite corners of your eyes. In addition, maintain a few extra yards' distance from your man. This will give you an added split-second to get a look at the ball *without* his moving behind you.

As the ball comes closer, you can then move to close him down. Until that point, however, being too near is a liability, not an advantage.

**Practice**—Ball-watching is a common flaw. To improve your vision as a defender, have a game with five to seven players per team plus goalies on a half field. Use *two* soccer balls. The extra ball will force all athletes—especially those defending—to develop 360° awareness. It will foster the good habit of looking around the entire field whenever your man is without a ball.

## JOCKEYING THE BALL CARRIER

The term *jockeying* means maintaining a good defensive position on the ball carrier while denying him a specific route to your goal. For example, if he's right-footed, you might want to force him to move toward his left. You do this by standing toward his right side at an angle.

As you retreat, your weight should be balanced and on the balls of your feet, not your heels. Knees are slightly bent, and your eyes are on the ball.

Just because your opponent has the ball doesn't mean you can't fake him out of it. As you bend forward from your waist, lurch your shoulders and head toward him *without* altering your center of gravity or balance. Do this to convince him that you're about to lunge in for a tackle.

At worst, your fake will be a distraction, designed to cause the ball carrier to lose sight of what's happening around him. He may fail to notice open teammates.

At best, your foe might panic. He could be lured into making an awkward move to avoid your "tackle," causing him to lose the ball. This way you avoid the inherent risk in tackling, yet you've managed to win the ball back for your team.

**Practice**—Set up two opposite lines of players, approximately 40 yards apart. The attackers are just inside the midfield stripe, with the defenders on the goalline.

The server is next to the attackers' line. He starts the action by kicking a ball between the two groups. The front player from each line then sprints forward.

If the attacker arrives at the ball first, the defender must jockey him until he forces the attacker to run out of room toward the sideline or wins the ball.

It is important that the defender sprint at full speed toward his man before the attacker gains possession. If he fails to close him down, the opponent's job will be made far easier. He'll be allowed to advance without pressure. This enables the attacker to dribble at or near full speed.

However, the defender must not rush at his man mindlessly. After the attacker has gained control of the ball and is closed down with the defender a few yards from him, the defender should start retreating at approximately the same speed as the dribbler is advancing. Through effective jockeying, he can eventually slow the ball carrier. At this point the defender has gained the advantage.

My teammate Ken Fogarty (#7) always draws the toughest marking assignments, such as former Cosmos star Giorgio Chinaglia. It's tough and unglamorous work. (Jon Van Woerden)

To practice variety and decision-making, have the server strike balls at different paces. Sometimes the defender should get to the ball first. When this happens, it's his job to pass the ball back to the server. In other words, the attacker has become the defender and the defender is now the attacker, just as in a real game.

Not only will you learn to use vital defensive skills, but you'll also find your judgment tested. When deciding when to challenge for a ball, the defender must be aware of the risks of failure. You'll learn to be cautious, just as you should be in a real game.

Incidentally, I recommend using goalies with this drill. Should the attacker get past his rival, he is rewarded with a try at goal. And, just as in a game, he must take the chance quickly.

## TACKLING

If all goes as planned, solid marking and intelligent jockeying will cause the other team to lose possession. However, no matter how strong your defense, there will be times when you must go for the ball. That's when it's time to tackle.

Tackling is the series of movements made by a defender to regain the ball. It involves making contact with the ball first. *You must remove the ball from the man, not the man from the ball.* However, physical contact is permitted if you are judged to be playing the ball. You may even mount a shoulder-to-shoulder charge when the ball is within playing distance, about one yard.

**Technique**—Generally, you should tackle so the inside of your foot strikes the ball. Your supporting foot should be firmly planted in the ground and your weight is forward. Get your shoulders and the knee of your tackling foot over the ball. That foot moves downward and hits just above the ball's center. If you strike the lower portion of the ball, an experienced rival will lift it over your foot.

Your tackling foot moves downward and "locks" behind the ball. When you are in this position, there is no way that the opponent can advance the ball past you.

The most important factors in winning a tackle are leverage, balance, technique, determination and timing. You must "want" the ball more than the attacker does. You can't both own it.

## DEFENSIVE STRATEGY

Certainly, if your team lacks offensive skills, great defense won't be enough to compensate. However, if you really want to become a good player, you need to become a good defensive performer.

Defense involves a lot more than just regaining the ball. The primary objective is to prevent the other team from scoring.

That sounds obvious, but too many players seem to forget it. In their rush to gain possession, they may gamble and make mistakes. A great number of goals are needlessly made because a defensive player lost a challenge for the ball and was out of position as his man advanced past him to attack.

A Vancouver Whitecaps defender (right) uses the inside of his foot to tackle the ball away from Ray Hudson. (Steve Merzer)

**Controlled Aggression**—A good defensive player uses *controlled* aggression. If he sees a chance to get the ball, he'll take it. But he'll not take dumb risks that involve more risk than he can gain.

Furthermore, he'll analyze the situation. A smart challenge near the opponents' goal may not be an intelligent challenge in midfield. If you get beaten in your opponents' penalty area, they still have about 90 yards to advance before reaching your goal. And your teammates have plenty of time to adjust. However, if you're beaten in your half of the pitch, your opponents might be only 40 yards from your goal.

Experience will teach you when, and when not, to attempt a tackle. If you study a professional match, you'll notice how rarely defenders actually try to win the ball, especially in their own half of the field. They're far more likely to retreat, stay with their men, and wait for the attacking side to attempt a difficult pass.

Good defense is often denying the attackers the easy options, forcing them to *earn* their advance. Sooner or later, they'll make a mistake *if* you've taken all the easy options away from them.

However, if in your impatience you expose yourself to a silly tackle and are beaten, the entire balance changes. Now the ball carrier is free and can run at your goal without pressure. If a fellow defender comes to mark him, that will probably leave another attacker free, most likely in a dangerous position.

**Practice** — One way to develop this skill is with a partner. Place the ball on the ground between you. On a signal, both of you try to tackle the ball.

A word on injuries is appropriate at this point. It's not unusual for some kids to be intimidated by bigger kids. Instead of going full-force into a tackle, they stick their foot in half-heartedly. By not using body weight, they've *increased* the chance of injury. An all-out effort is the best and safest way to win the ball.

**TACKLING DRILL**
Players should lean forward and strike downward on the middle of the ball. (Jim Frank)

The sliding tackle is perhaps the most spectacular defensive skill in soccer.
(Stan Green)

## SLIDING TACKLE

The sliding tackle is certainly the most spectacular method of regaining possession. But it's really a last resort to make up for a preceding defensive error. You'll need to use it when you are not in a good defensive position and have to make a *desperate* maneuver to recover.

Just because you may be beaten does not mean a sliding tackle is in order. You should never use it unless you're virtually certain of success. If you fail, you'll be flat on your back, out of the play, and useless to your team. It's usually better to let someone else pick up your man so you can move to a central position behind the ball.

**Technique**—The sliding tackle is used most often when you are running next to—and in the same direction as—the ball carrier. When the ball is ahead of him, slide your body and sweep your kicking foot across his path. Be sure to deflect the ball wide, not back into his shins! Use your instep, if possible.

Do not attempt a sliding tackle if you're behind your man. Doing this is not only a foul, but very dangerous too. You're objective is to win the game, not cripple an opponent. Referees are usually strict on this, even if the player is making an honest attempt to play the ball.

Ray Hudson (left) using the sliding tackle. Notice how he is ready to come across the ball to poke it away from the attacker without committing a foul. (Steve Merzer)

## TEAM DEFENSE: THE TRANSITION GAME

Many a game has been won or lost by how quickly a team makes the transition from offense to defense. Two critical factors determine success.

First, when attacking, you and your teammates must be aware of the consequences of all your actions. If a large number of you are ahead of the ball, hoping for a forward pass, you'll be stranded should the other team regain possession. Your team must maintain depth while attacking. This means that some players are ahead of the ball, some to the sides and most behind it.

In addition, the player in possession must be careful. If he's playing the ball *square,* or backward, he must be certain his pass will not be intercepted. Does that mean you should always pass forward? No, but it does mean that you must be aware of the chance of success of each pass. Weigh the potential reward of success against the consequences of failure.

Second is what happens in the critical seconds after the ball is lost. If the opponent who intercepts the pass or wins the tackle is allowed to play the ball forward quickly, your team may be in trouble. As best you can, one of your players must slow him down, forcing him to dribble or pass sideways or backward. If he's allowed to advance the ball upfield at full speed, your side will not have enough defenders behind the ball.

Furthermore, the player on your team who moves to slow down the ball carrier must do just that. If he takes a silly risk and challenges unsuccessfully for possession only to be beaten, your defense will probably find itself outnumbered and overrun.

**Practice**—One of the best ways to learn the transition game is the small-sided game. Incorporate "forced marking" into your contests. That is, each of you is responsible for a specific opponent when your side is defending. As soon as your team loses the ball, you have to mark that player.

You can even add the condition that you are allowed to tackle only that specific opponent—and he's allowed to tackle only you. You'll soon find that your transition game in full-sided contests will improve.

## SUPPORTING

In most cases, especially when you've executed the fundamentals of the transition game properly, you will enjoy a numerical advantage when defending. When that's the case, a free man can be used to support the teammate who is marking the ball carrier. This impedes the attacker's route to the goal, forcing him to either beat two men, or move backward or sideways.

If you're *supporting,* you want to be far enough from your teammate that the attacker can't beat both of you with the same move. However, you want to be close enough that you can close him down as soon as he advances around your teammate. In general, you should be about five yards away and on the side closer to your goal.

Communication is vital. If the defender who is marking the ball carrier knows he has support, he can attempt a tackle instead of retreating. When I'm covering the ball carrier, I usually hear my teammate Ken Fogarty exclaiming, "Have a bite Rocky, I'm right behind you." By that, he means to challenge for the ball when appropriate because even if I fail, he's there to provide cover.

If we have the attacker isolated, Ken will instruct me to force him to the right or left. I will then jockey him in that direction, *toward* Ken's position. At that point, Ken will have little trouble winning the ball. Often called *double marking,* this technique is demonstrated on the next page.

If you are supporting, you must be aware of what is happening on the ball and around it. Don't have a "one-track mind," neglecting to see opponents making penetrating runs behind you.

## DEFENDING AGAINST SET PIECES

One of the toughest situations presented to any defense occurs when a free kick is awarded either in your penalty area or just outside the front of that zone. According to the laws of the game, the attacking team need not wait for a whistle before putting the ball in play. This means that you must set up as soon as possible.

## DOUBLE MARKING

1) Use double marking to lure the attacker into the your defense's "trap." The marker (partially hidden at right) forces the dribbler to move to his left.

2) To the attacker's left is a supporting defender.

3) The supporting defender comes up to the ball and takes it away. (Jim Frank)

However, should a member of the attacking team ask the referee to move all defenders at least 10 yards from the ball, play will be stopped and not restarted until the referee signals.

**The Wall** — Depending on the danger presented by a direct or indirect shot on goal, the defending unit may wish to use the *wall*. This human blockade can include from 2 to 10 players. Except for an indirect kick right in front of your goal and in the penalty area, it's very rare for a wall to use more than five men. The reason is obvious — if you place too many defenders in your wall, there will be unguarded attackers. They could be more dangerous than the free kick itself.

Your goalkeeper must decide whether to erect a wall and, if so, how many players to use. The wall is responsible for blocking the near side of the goal while the keeper covers the far side. To be effective, the outside man in the wall should stand on an imaginary line that connects the ball and the near post. All teammates in the wall line up next to him, shoulder to shoulder.

It is essential that those in the wall have sufficient courage not to allow the ball to pass through them. With rare exception, such a mistake is punished by a goal, the goalie being both out of position and having his vision blocked.

There are two ways to line up the wall. A forward may be used to stand upfield of the ball and align the outside man, called the *wall captain*.

Another option is for the goalie to position the wall. He moves to the near post and directs the wall captain. The wall captain faces his goalie until he is properly positioned. At that point, he makes sure his teammates have formed a solid wall.

A wall of white-shirted players help defend the near side of their goal again this free kick. (Jim Frank)

When using this method, the goalie must be alert. If the opponents on the ball set up quickly, they may take the shot as you stand yelling directions at the near post, 24 unguarded feet of goal to your side!

As the level of soccer improves, so does the complexity of set plays you'll face on restarts. As such, it's imperative that you have an adequate number of players in defensive positions. If five men are required in the wall, and the other team is pushing several players forward, it's the goalie's job to instruct *all* of his teammates to get back. Most of those not in the wall should protect the territory in front of your goal rather than mark specific opponents.

**Corner Kicks**—These present another problem. Obviously, you want to cover each opponent who is in your attacking third. Except for the kicker—from whom all defenders must stay 10 yards—this involves having a defender mark a specific rival.

The basic principles of defense apply on corner kicks. For example, if you're marking an opponent who is at the top of your penalty area—18 yards from your goal—chances are he'll make a run toward your net just before the ball is kicked. For you to see both him and the ball, give him sufficient room and positon yourself in the path between him and your goal.

On the other hand, if he's lined up near your net, you must mark him tighter.

The goalkeeper is your "field coach." It is his responsibility to make certain all opponents are covered *before* the other team is ready to put the ball back in play. In addition, one defender should stand next to the near post. It is his duty to prevent the ball from passing between him and that post. Remember, a corner kick is direct, so a kicker imparting swerve may shoot the ball into your goal.

Some teams like to place a second defender at the far post. Should your goalie leave his line to attempt to intercept the cross, the two players on the posts move inward to cover the vacated goal.


**PENALTY KICK**

When a penalty kick is awarded, only your goalie can save you. However, it is important that all defenders know what to do should the shot hit a goalpost or crossbar or be knocked back into play by your goalie.

If the first occurs, the kicker may not touch the ball a second time until it has been played by at least one other player. However, once the ball has touched the goalie—or anyone else—it's in play for all to kick.

Remember that no member of either team—except the shooter and the goalie—may be in the penalty box or arc before the ball is struck. However, once the shot is made, there are no restrictions on player movement. If there's a loose ball, you want to get to it first. You should have several defenders positioned on the edge of the penalty area, ready to charge as soon as the shot is taken.

If you're a defender and you get to the ball first, don't attempt anything fancy. There will be no time to pivot with the ball to make a pass or an upfield clearance. Doing either creates unnecessary risks. Instead, just push the ball over the nearest boundary line. It's better to yield a corner kick or throw-in than to take chances in front of your goal.

**For the Goalie**—As for you goalies, you have my sympathy. I know of no situation in team sports in which the odds are so heavily stacked. You're not allowed to move until the shot is taken and at least a part of each of your feet must be in contact with the goalline until that happens.

About all you can do is guess where the ball is going. As the ball is kicked, step slightly forward and then push off in that direction. Except for a rare lucky miss or a mishit, you'll stand little chance. Just do the best you can. Should you be fortunate enough to reach the ball, but are unable to catch it, deflect it as wide as possible. It's now up to your defenders to do the rest.

## OFFSIDE TRAP

The offside trap is an advanced maneuver that may confuse young players. It's my belief that you should start and stay with the fundamentals for a long time. Don't use this type of tactical stuff until your skills are refined.

The purpose of the offside trap is to pull an opponent—or opponents—offside. You do this by having defenders off the ball advance upfield so at least one member of the attacking team is offside when the ball is played forward by one of his teammates. Even if their forwards are alert and retreat to avoid being offside, you've taken them farther from your goal, pushing them backward.

On signal—usually a spoken code word from a specific defender or the goalkeeper—all members of the defending team who are behind the front attackers must sprint forward. They must do this instantly. Should one lag, the opponents would remain onside and the defensive team would be hopelessly out of position.

There are certain instances in which an offside trap is automatic. For example, when the defense clears the ball upfield, the team should move forward together to force the attackers to vacate the penalty area—and, if possible, the entire attacking third. Another time is when their striker is isolated several yards ahead of his teammates and does not have the ball. The defenders would move together to leave him in an offside position.

The referee will not blow his whistle until the ball has been played forward with an attacker in an offside position. Thus, an alert ball carrier will not pass the ball forward if he sees a teammate offside. You defenders can't relax, thinking your job is over.

Equally important, your victim must be in a central position or in front of the ball. If you trap an attacker who is not considered to have gained an advantage by being offside, no violation has occurred and play will continue.

It's important that you understand how an offense should counter your trap. In most cases, their forwards will retreat. A withdrawn player—such as a defender or midfielder—runs toward your goal and through a gap in your backline. Just before that person penetrates, a pass should be struck into the space behind you. If timed right, their player will be behind your defenders as the ball arrives with only the goalie to beat. Since he was in an onside position at the moment the pass was struck, he is not considered offside even though the ball arrives with him behind all your outfield players.

It sounds complex, and it is. That's why I suggest you leave this tactic to advanced players. It's a maneuver that works only if all players understand all of the components of the trap, how it's countered, and how to counter the counters!

## OVERVIEW

Except for the offside trap, defense really isn't very complicated. It's based on a few basic principles combined with a lot of common sense, determination and practice.

Many of the offensive practice drills I've described also encourage defensive skills. That's something all players should have, including forwards and midfielders.

# CHAPTER EIGHT

# Goalkeeping

In my NASL career, I've had the honor of playing with two world-class goalkeepers—Gordon Banks and Jan van Beveren. Playing with them opened my eyes to the difference between good goalkeepers and great goalkeepers. Great goalies make big saves that are the difference between winning and losing.

No matter how good your defense, the opposition will get good scoring chances. That's why it's essential to have a goalie that consistently makes exceptional plays. He will lift your spirits while deflating the opposition's. Without exception, a successful team has a fine goalie.

In my experience, van Beveren made the Strikers an exceptional team rather than just a good one. Playing behind a defense that was, at best, inconsistent, he made dozens of unbelievable saves. That allowed players like me, Gerd and Nene to do our business at the other end against lesser goalies.

Teams can win with a mediocre defender or two, an average wing or even just a hard-working striker of above-average skill. But no team will go far without super goalkeeping.

This is true for soccer at all levels—from Saturday morning leagues to World Cup Finals. If everything else is even, the side with the better goalie will win three times out of four. In my native England, as of this writing, the highest paid player is goalie Peter Shilton—and rightly so.

Bravery is a characteristic of all goalies. (Stan Green)

## NECESSARY CHARACTERISTICS

What is it that makes great goalies like Shilton, Banks, van Beveren and Birkenmeier so special? Actually, it's a variety of ingredients.

First, a goalie must be a talented athlete. Either you're born that way or you're not. It's as simple as that.

However, that's the only aspect of goalkeeping that you can't learn or practice through determination and work. Other very important factors are intelligence, courage, leadership and a willingness to work harder than your counterparts. Unlike some other positions, goalkeeping requires as much mental skill as physical skill.

**Determination**—Of all the positions in soccer, playing the net is the one in which determination seems to carry the most weight. I've seen average talents become outstanding performers simply because of an eagerness to excel. It seems that a goalie can improve more rapidly and more thoroughly than other players if he has the will to do so.

All great goalies are that way. In our club, van Beveren and Banks were always the last ones off the practice field. They seemed to torture themselves in training, working on all aspects of their craft with a fervor that's hard to describe.

**Dominant Presence**—In addition, they were willing to do more than just stand between the goalposts. They *dominated* the entire penalty area. I can't tell you how many times opposition forwards misfired on close-in shots because they were so concerned that Jan or Gordon would make a miraculous save. The strikers either tried a shot in the corner of the net or put excess pace on the ball.

As a result, what should have scoring shots would often sail harmlessly over the crossbar or around the post. Just the threat of greatness made Jan and Gordon even greater.

**Physical Characteristics**—A goalie must be tall enough to win crosses in the air, yet not so lanky as to be vulnerable to low shots. Most outstanding goalies are between 5-feet 10-inches and 6-feet 3-inches. Naturally, there are some exceptions to the rule, but not many.

All are agile and quick. They possess good hand/eye coordination, too.

**Mental Characteristics**—A goalie must be smart about the game. He needs to be aware of what's happening around the ball, as well as provide "coaching on the field." This type of understanding and anticipation develops through experience.

A goalie must be a leader, constantly directing teammates and providing moral support.

Courage is also vital. You need guts to throw yourself into a pile of swinging feet in pursuit of the ball. You need the nerve to take charge and intercept passes. It means being able to live with mistakes and maintain a confident air, even when things go wrong.

If you're a goalie, you must learn to handle failure, refusing to let it better you. Sooner or later all goalies have bad games. Sometimes a bunch of goals will be scored against you because of your defense's shortcomings. As goalie you must take some of the blame, rightly or wrongly, when goals are scored.

You have to accept it as part of the hazards of the position and try to learn from mistakes. That's possible when you're a veteran goalie with many years of experience. But it's not easy if you're a young player who makes a mistake that costs your team a game. I've seen many promising goalies hurt by such experiences, especially when teammates and coaches aren't sympathetic and supportive. That's as true in the pros as it is in the schoolyards.


## STRATEGY FOR ALL PLAYERS

I strongly recommend that *all* young players try playing goalie. Also, nobody should play that position exclusively at the youth level. (In fact, no player younger than 13 should play one position exclusively.)

A young goalie should have some field experience to learn strategy and skill. You'll also learn about controlling the ball with just your feet. Advanced-level goalies are often called upon to make saves with their feet or leave the penalty area to beat an opponent to a loose ball.

You'll find that most top goalies are skilled enough to play any position. When injuries put several Cosmo forwards out of commission one season, goalie Birkenmeier responded. He not only played up front, but he scored goals, too.

**Concentrate on Basics**—Diving saves are generally not recommended for players younger than 13. Also, simply stopping shots may create lingering bad habits. It's better to work on the basics that can be done correctly, such as catching the ball.

For these reasons, I've divided the remainder of this chapter into two segments: 1) skills and drills for all goalies, and 2) activities designed exclusively for intermediate and advanced goalies.

## CATCHING THE BALL

The one distinguishing characteristic of playing goal is that you are allowed to use your hands and arms to control the ball. The necessary skills have as much in common with basketball or baseball as the skills of your teammates. Many fine American goalies—such as foreword-writer Alan Mayer—starred in the so-called "traditional" sports before taking up soccer.

**"W" Catch**—The technique of catching a soccer ball is different from that used in any other game. On all saves *not* made within the plane of your body, your fingers form a sort of web or "W" behind the ball. As shown in the accompanying photo, the thumbs and index fingers are spread behind the ball. Not only does this make catching shots easier, but it also guarantees that any misplays will drop the ball in front of you, not through your hands and into the goal.

**W CATCH**
When catching the ball to your side or above your body, use this type of catch, as described in the text. (Jim Frank)

**W-Catch Practice**—The W catch must become second nature. You learn it best through practice and repetition. Find a fellow goalie and stand 5 to 10 yards apart. Toss the ball back and forth, providing each other with a variety of catches to execute. Don't throw the ball hard. The idea is to get in the habit of catching the ball correctly.

If you like, you can dropkick the ball, taking turns as server and saver. This way, the server can be working on a skill, too.

**Soft Hands**—As you get better, you'll discover that shots become more and more powerful. To eventually be able to hold onto a ball traveling up to 70 miles per hour, you'll need to develop "soft" hands. Just as with trapping, think of the ball as an egg. As it arrives, withdraw your hands to cradle it without breaking the shell.

**Soft-Hands Practice**—To practice soft hands, stand 5 to 10 yards from a practice partner. Toss the ball back and forth using just one hand to make the catch. This forces you to get that hand in a good position to control the ball. Also, you can work on withdrawing that hand on impact. Of course, you must watch the ball all the way into your hand.

As your skill improves, add this new, and more difficult, twist. As shown in the accompanying photo, both goalies are playing "catch" with one hand while the other supports their body weight. You can also do this with your chest facing down in a modified push-up position.

Either way, make sure you practice with both hands. It's important for goalies to develop equal skill catching and diving to the left and right. "One-sided" goalies don't get very far in soccer. Skillful opponents will challenge your weakness without mercy.

To improve hand/eye coordination along with "touch," lie on your back. Toss the ball and catch it with one hand.

**PARTNER PRACTICE**
Improve soft hands and concentration with drills like this. (Jim Frank)

**STOMACH PRACTICE**
This drill increases flexibility. It's important that the goalie uses two hands
to catch the ball in this exercise to avoid forming bad habits. (Jim Frank)

**On-Your-Stomach Practice**—You can enhance flexibility and hand/eye coordination by practicing on your stomach. Have a server a few yards away kick the ball at you. You must stretch to get both hands to catch the ball. Don't use just one hand. It's better to practice correctly and drop the ball a few times than to catch a serve with one hand.

You can also have a third person grasp your ankles during this drill. This forces you to stretch from the waist to make the catch. Arch your back to get maximum benefit from the drill.

**Using Your Body**—Not all shots require a diving save. Many will be right at you. Contrary to popular belief, these are not easy to catch, especially if the ball is kicked powerfully.

If the shot arrives between waist and shoulder height, lean forward with your arms outstretched. Allow the ball to strike your chest as your arms surround its far side. There are two good reasons to lean forward. First, the shot is likely to be rising so you want your chest to be perpendicular to the ball's line of flight. In addition, if you miss the catch, your chest will direct the ball downward, directly in front of you. This gives you a second chance to grab it as it bounces back up.

If the ball is rolling, place your palms on the ground, face up. As you lean forward, the ball will roll up your arms and into your upper body. Cradle the ball firmly against your chest.

These techniques are very important. Whenever possible, a good goalie gets his body directly behind the ball. This prevents mishandled shots from sneaking into the net. Every goalie has seen a seemingly easy shot sail through his fingertips. It will happen to you, too, so get your body into position to back up your hands.

**BODY WORK**
Your arms should surround the ball as you pull it into your chest. (Jim Frank)

## HIGH SHOTS

Outdoor soccer has more high balls lofted into the penalty area than does the indoor game. Most indoor shots are low because the crossbar and width of the net are smaller. This makes heading practically a lost art indoors, but this is not true with outdoor soccer.

The regulation outdoor goal is eight feet high. To be a good goalie, you must be able to intercept crosses at the highest possible point. Essentially, this is above the height at which an outfield player could leap to head the ball. In the pros and college, that's often above the crossbar.

When you've come off your line to narrow the shooter's angle, the goal becomes "taller." But if you're only six yards from your goal, it's possible for a skilled finisher to loft a ball well above the eight-feet mark. The ball can pass over you before descending under the crossbar.

**What You Need**—Saving such high shots and intercepting crosses involves judgment, leaping ability and timing.

Judgment is essential, especially on crosses. You must determine early where the ball will enter your catching range. You need to arrive at that spot as the ball does. If you get there too late, not only won't you make the play, but you'll also be out of position to save any shot. Conversely, arriving early will force you to jump from a standing start, hampering your leaping ability.

Jumping ability derives from powerful legs. To develop powerful muscles I suggest plenty of running and a modest amount of weight lifting. In some countries goalies spend much time making practice saves in the sand. Having to push off against soft surfaces develops the muscles needed for jumping and diving.

Timing is important. As noted, you want to be at the apex of your leap as you make the catch. The farther above opponents you grab the ball, the less interference you'll experience making the W catch.

When leaping, particularly in heavy traffic, a lot of goalies place one knee in front of their body prior to takeoff. Lifting that leg aids their momentum before they push off with the opposite foot.

Having a knee in front of your body will discourage overzealous forwards from playing *you,* rather than the ball. However, if you're judged by the referee to be using that knee as a weapon, he will call a foul against you.

Cosmos star Hubert Birkenmeier "watches" the ball into his hands and uses the W catch to bring it under control. (Jann Zlotkin)

When intercepting crosses, catch the ball above the heads of the leaping defenders and attackers. (Stan Green)

## PUNCHING THE BALL

Sometimes there are so many players near the ball that attempting to catch it would risk dropping it. In this case, it's best to be safe and deflect the ball toward the least dangerous area. To do this, use your fist, or fists.

When punching the ball, also called *boxing the ball,* you have certain priorities. Here's the order: height, width and distance. You must strike just under the center of the ball, using an upward motion with your hands.

You want to aim it upfield, placing it as wide as possible. Redirect it toward the side of the field that's closer to you. Never aim for the far-post side.

You need to get the ball far away from your goal. This comes with timing and by striking close to the ball's center, slightly underneath it, with your knuckles. Don't try to "kill" the ball with a knockout punch. You might miss it entirely.

**Punching Technique**—Sometimes you should punch the ball with one fist. At other times you need to use both fists. Different situations require different techniques.

When you are boxing the ball back in the direction from which it came, use two fists. Keep knuckles parallel to the ground when using both fists.

Use one hand to punch when you want to keep the ball going in the same direction. This can happen when a cross arrives with you near the back post. You should also use one fist when you want to alter the ball's course slightly. For example, do this if you're in front of the goal's center and you wish to aim the ball upfield toward the touchline it's moving toward. With this technique, keep knuckles perpendicular to the turf.

**PUNCHING**
Position your hands like this when using one or two fists to punch the ball. (Jim Frank)

**PUNCHING**
When punching the ball, your priorities are to hit the ball high, wide and far. (Jim Frank)

## TIPPING SHOTS OVER THE CROSSBAR

You don't have to catch every high shot moving toward the net. In fact, trying to catch every high shot can be dangerous—especially if you miss. When you have doubt about being able to catch the ball, don't try. In most cases, lightly touching the ball's underside will deflect it over the bar.

**Deflecting Technique**—Use an open hand with palm facing up just lower than your fingertips. As the ball meets your hand, push the ball upward.

An open hand provides a greater surface area and control than a fist. If you try to punch the ball over the bar, you run the risk of skimming the ball off your knuckles without changing its direction. Use your fist only when aiming the ball within the field of play and when you need to strike the ball far.

**Exception**—When you're far from your goalline and the ball is dipping, punch it far. It will be too high and behind you to be catchable, and you are too far from the goal to deflect it over the crossbar. In this case, use two fists to punch. If you have to stretch far to reach the ball, use one hand.

**High-Shot Practice**—Two servers can play a series of crosses and shots into the goal area. Work with a server (perhaps taking corner kicks) and two to four attackers who are positioned in front of the goal. It's their job to put the ball in the net. It's yours to prevent that. Because reacting to close-in shots is a hit-and-miss (mostly miss) proposition, you must be aggressive in cutting off crosses.

If your footwork needs improvement, especially when backpedaling, have a server stand 20 to 30 yards directly in front of your goal. He rolls a ball that you must run to, scoop up and return. As this happens, the server lobs a ball over your head. You must retreat *without* turning sideways or facing your goal.

As you backpedal, do not allow your feet to cross. Remain square to the flight of the incoming shot at all times and keep your eyes on it. Use your best judgment and either catch the ball, deflect it over the bar or punch it away.

Whenever possible, catch the ball. Challenge yourself. Don't take "the easy way out," particularly in practice.

Another practice method is to play a small-sided game in which all goals must be headed into the net. Your coach should scale the field proportionately in length (but *not* width) to the number of participants. You'll get plenty of work—under simulated match conditions—on your aerial game.

**TIPPING**
At left is the hand position to use to tip a ball over the crossbar. At right, notice how goalkeeper Wes Reinhardt's fingers are higher than his palm. This gives plenty of hand surface to redirect the ball over the bar. (Jim Frank)

## OVERVIEW

Up to this point we've covered the basics of goalkeeping that most goalies, young and mature, can do. These skills are vital and basic. The best learning tool is repetition. Catching the ball in the W of your fingers and using your body as a backup should eventually be instinctive. You have enough to think about during a game without worrying about how to catch the ball.

**A Word to Coaches**—However, coaches must remember that young goalies have limited attention spans coupled with a desire for fun playing experiences. Repetitive practice drills do not meet either of those criteria. I've seen far too many promising goalies "burn out" because of criticism and lack of fun.

I suggest working on basic techniques for a few minutes at a time. A goalie has years to develop technique. Don't try to make him master his craft in one hour!

Excessive repetition is boring, and boredom causes a breakdown in concentration. That, in turn, leads to sloppy technical execution and bad habits.

## ADVANCED GOALKEEPING TECHNIQUES

Not until your body starts maturing will you be able to generate sufficient leg power to dive for the ball. There is no set age at which you'll be ready. We develop at different times. However, in most cases, if you're not 13 years old, you're probably not ready to attempt this skill. You're better off waiting until you can do it properly rather than risk injury or bad habits.

## DIVING

You must dive for a ball when a shot arrives to your side, too far to reach without leaving your feet. There are many types of diving saves, but all have some common technique.

**Basic Technique**—Your hands should arrive to the point where they'll catch the ball as soon as possible. Your body will naturally follow your hands. A lot of goalies incorrectly dive and *then* move their hands toward the ball. This is too little, too late.

There are two methods for saving low shots. One is for balls aimed just inside the post. The other is for those near your body.

For the first type, use your near-side hand to lead you into your dive. It should be a few inches above the ground to meet the middle of the ball, with your palm facing the field of play. Your far-side hand will come over the top of the ball, pushing it down.

As you make the catch, three of the ball's four "sides" are protected. Your hands cover the back and top, and the turf in contact with its underside. As soon as possible, bring the ball into your stomach and grasp it firmly against your body.

The most difficult save is catching a fast shot that is on the ground about two to three feet from your side. If the shooter is a few yards away, you may need to use your foot to make a desperation kick save. However, if possible, try to catch the ball rather than yielding a rebound.

To do this, kick your near-side foot in the *opposite* direction of your dive. In other words, if you're diving to your right, your right foot moves to your left. This enables your body to collapse quickly. Get your hands down rapidly and use the W catch.

## PARRYING THE BALL

Some shots will arrive just at the limits of your reach. When this happens, you'll only be able to get the fingertips of one hand on the ball. A catch isn't possible. Instead, deflect the shot wide of the post and, if possible, over the goalline. It is far better to concede a corner kick than to miss a catch. Be safe, not sorry.

**Technique**—To parry shots, angle your palm so that the ball strikes it before touching your fingertips. Your near-side hand leads your body into its dive. Your body should be parallel to the turf and on the same plane as the incoming shot.

For high shots, those above the plane at which your body can dive, use your far-side hand. It moves across your shoulders and propels the ball wide or over the goal.

**ONE-HAND PARRY**
The goalkeeper keeps his eyes glued to the ball until he's redirected it. (Jim Frank)

## DIVING PRACTICE

Diving is not natural for most people, so don't be discouraged if it takes you some time to get good at it. As stated earlier, incorrect form may be punished by pain. Hard ground knows no manners. Rather than risking injury, practice on a soft surface. A beach or gym mats are good alternatives to hard ground. A spongy surface will also force your legs to work harder to get maximum thrust, building leg muscles.

You might think that the best practice is to face lots of tough shots. That's true only if your technique is already outstanding. Even if you're a successful goalie, you may not have good form. If so, you won't progress as you get older. Your shortcomings will be exposed. Do not get in the habit of parrying balls that you could catch. In training, work on holding onto those shots.

**Diving Drill #1 —** If diving from a standing start is giving you trouble, use the progression method. Start on your knees and have a server flip balls that you must dive to reach.

Next, begin in the catcher's squat. When, and if, you can dive correctly from that position, you are ready to work from a normal stance.

**DIVING DRILL #1**
A good way to learn to dive to your side correctly is to start from a catcher's squat with a server gently tossing "shots" to *both* sides. (Jim Frank)

**Diving Drill #2** — Here's another good warmup drill to enhance technical development: With a server nearby, a teammate kneels on all fours (with head tucked under for safety). You, the goalie, stand to his side. The ball is then tossed to the opposite side of the "obstacle." You must dive over him and catch the ball cleanly.

Perform this drill in sets of no more than 10 saves while concentrating on maintaining good form and adhering to goalkeeping's basic principles — web catch, watching the ball into your hands and landing with your hands on top of the ball.

As always, spend more time working on your weaker side.

**Somersault Drills** — You can improve both balance and diving ability by incorporating some gymnastics. Stand by one goalpost while facing the other. With a server poised on the penalty spot, do a somersault across the face of the goal. Just as you come to your feet, the server kicks a shot along the ground toward the far post. You dive and make the save.

Repeat the procedure in the opposite direction. Don't execute more than 10 saves per turn.

You can use somersaults to improve hand/eye coordination and to work on making difficult reflex saves on point-blank shots. For the former, throw the ball high in the air, do your somersault and try to catch the ball before it hits the ground.

**DIVING DRILL #2**
The diving over drill forces the keeper to execute a powerful push off with his near-sided leg. (Jim Frank)

To improve reaction time, stand in the middle of your goal, facing the server who is on the penalty spot. Do a front somersault. As you are about to regain your feet, the server dropkicks a hard shot for you to save. Don't worry about form in this situation, just block the ball. If possible, catch it. If not, deflect it into the least-dangerous position.

Another variation on the same theme is the *About-Face Drill*. With the server in the same starting position, stand on your goalline but with your back to him. As he yells "Turn!" you pivot, find the ball and make the save.

## DIVING INTO FEET

At times you'll find yourself in a one-on-one situation with an opponent who has taken the ball past your last defender. If you just stand on your line, or merely narrow his angle by moving forward slightly, he'll easily kick the ball into the goal.

Instead, you should offer the smallest amount of goal to the opponent while pressuring him as much as possible. You do this by moving forward to meet the ball.

**Technique**—Advance rapidly, under control. If you sprint at an experienced finisher and are running upright, he'll see that you aren't ready to get low. He'll shoot as you are in full stride, placing the ball on the ground where it would be toughest for you to reach.

As you move toward him, keep your hands low and be on your toes, ready to change direction instantly, if needed. Concentrate on the ball, and don't fall prey to head or shoulder fakes.

**ONE-ON-ONE**
1) When you are goalie and find yourself in a one-on-one attack, try to get as close to the attacker as possible.

You want the pressure to induce panic, perhaps causing him to dribble the ball too far forward. If that happens, pounce on that loose ball as if you own it. Be smart, aggressive and brave. Anything less will result in a goal.

If the ball carrier is advancing from an angle, you can use your near goalpost as an ally. Use your upper body and fully outstretched arms to cover the near side. If you can force him to abruptly change direction and move wider, he may lose the ball over the goalline, or be forced to shoot from a difficult angle.

There will be occasions in which you will find yourself racing him for a through pass that's rolling toward you. If you can beat him to it, dive on the ball with your body parallel to your goal. Should you be a split-second late and realize that you'll arrive just after his shot, you must do the same technique but leave your feet early so your body hits the ground *as* he's striking the ball. Throw yourself across his path, getting as close to the shot as possible. Your objective is to block the goal with your body, making his shot strike you.

There are several of ways to improve this unpleasant, but important, aspect of goalkeeping:

**Breakaway Drills**—You can have a server, positioned next to the attacker, about 35 yards from goal. Start a few yards off your line. The server kicks the ball forward. You must decide whether to try to win the ball, whether to dive into his feet as he shoots, or whether you should merely advance a few yards to decrease his shooting angle.

2) Hit the ground just as he's either shooting or trying to dribble around you. You must be quick *and* brave to be successful. (Stan Green)

A drill that practices bravery and technique begins with you in goal, holding the ball. A shooter stands poised at the edge of the penalty area. Roll the ball to him and sprint toward it. As he prepares to shoot, dive across the plane of the goal.

This is not an exercise for young goalies. It's too dangerous. And it certainly isn't one that any normal human being will enjoy. If you succeed, the ball will strike your body or arms after having been struck from a few feet away. You may even catch a foot in the process.

However, being able to make this type of save is important. You can be sure that an entire game will someday depend on such a play's outcome.

## DISTRIBUTION

Most people think that a goalie's only job is to stop shots. More correctly, that's his main job. However, once he's gained possession he becomes the first line of offense. He must then get the ball to one of his attacking teammates. This is called *distributing*.

Some goalies are so good at distributing the ball that their opponents are reluctant to commit too many players to attacking. This again proves that the best defense is a good offense.

There are two methods of distribution—throwing and kicking the ball.

**OVERHEAD**
The overhead throw combines distance with accuracy. (Stan Green)

## THROWING

When accuracy is most important, throw the ball. This is especially true when you have a teammate with room to move. Another situation is to deliver a pass when most members of the other team have retreated into their own half of the field. In this case, you can even roll the ball to a nearby teammate, usually one of your defenders.

**Different Tosses**—There are three types of tosses. The roll is the easiest for the receiver to control, but is useful only for short distances.

If you need to throw the ball farther, make a "baseball throw." It can be tough to play because the ball can skip, so don't use this method unless your receiver is wide open and has the skill to receive a tricky pass.

The third throw is the overhead. It travels farthest of the three. Start by standing sideways to your target. Cup the ball in the palm of your throwing hand and against your wrist. Bring it back to waist height. Sling your arm over the top as you release the ball, while your arm travels roughly perpendicular to the turf.

**ROLL**
The roll is best for short distributions. (Jim Frank)

**BASEBALL THROW**
The baseball throw is fine for intermediate distances. (Jim Frank)

## KICKING

A throw is the most accurate way to distribute the ball, but it's not always appropriate. When no one is in a good receiving position for your pass, it's best to get the ball as far upfield as possible. Generally, you should be able to kick a ball at least 10 to 25 yards farther than you can throw one.

There are two methods used by goalies—the drop kick and the punt.

**Drop-Kick Technique**—With rare exception, use a drop kick only when you want to either keep your kick low—such as when facing a strong wind—or get it to the receiver quickly. It's a more accurate way to distribute when kicking.

To drop kick, lean forward as you release the ball from the hand that's on the same side as your kicking foot. The knee of that leg is bent. Your supporting foot points at your target. Strike the ball with the instep as your toes face downward. A limited follow-through is all that's required.

A drop kick is only as safe as the ground is smooth. Although you strike the ball just after it hits the turf, a bad hop could cause a bad kick. Don't try it on uneven or muddy surfaces.

**Punting Technique**—A punt is safer. Even a bad punt will travel a good distance. This gives you time to get back in position if your opponents win possession.

The most important ingredient is an accurate and consistent drop. You want the ball to descend directly in front of your kicking foot. If you drop it to either side, you'll probably fail to strike it with your instep, causing you to lose distance and accuracy. If you drop it too close to your body, the result will be an "infield popup."

On the other hand, dropping it too far in front of you will cause you to hit the ball with the end of your shoe. This results in a low and short kick that, if intercepted, could present a significant danger.

**Practice**—To practice, kick a ball lightly into the goal. Work on consistent motion rather than just a fast foot swing. Meet the center of the ball with the instep—the "sweet spot"—of your foot to produce a lengthy kick.


## GAME SITUATIONS

Of course no goalkeeper can distribute the ball unless he has first won possession. The techniques described on the preceding pages represent only part of the equation.

You also have to be a smart goalie, one who can be in the right place at the right time and also think as a forward or a defender. Knowledge of the game leads to good anticipation. Most goalies get this way by having played other positions, too.

**Positioning**—One of the most significant but least appreciated aspects of goalkeeping is position. Great goalies do not have to leave their feet as often as other goalies because their positioning is usually perfect. When you need to make fewer spectacular saves, fewer dropped balls and rebounds result.

**PUNT**
Use the punt when you want to get the ball far upfield. (Jim Frank)

If you see a goalie making many great saves, ask yourself if he is compensating for bad positioning or "playing the crowd." That means making each save look special for the sake of drama.

You want to come off your line just enough to narrow the shooter's angle without leaving yourself vulnerable to a chip shot. The narrower the shooter's angle, the less you should leave your line. The closer he is to the goalline, the more likely he is to strike a cross. If you've come well off your line and are past the near post, you'll be out of position to intercept that service.

Another factor in angle play is whether your opponent is more likely to pass or shoot. If he has a teammate open for a pass on the opposite side of the goal, who is also in a good position to finish, you must be cautious about cutting down his angle.

The direction in which the ball is rolling is part of your decision. One that's rolling toward your opponent is easy for him to chip. One that's rolling away from him, toward you, is virtually impossible to loft into the net.

Doing it all correctly will come with experience. In other words, *you will make mistakes*, sometimes costing the game. That's why I have a special admiration for successful goalkeepers. They are strong individuals who survive emotionally draining experiences. They learn and grow from them.

# CHAPTER NINE

# The Mental Game

Soccer is a great game for many reasons. It offers physical challenges unlike any other sport. But often overlooked is the mental challenge soccer presents.

In other team sports, decision-making is a relatively minor part of the athlete's overall equation for success. A baseball player has a few options if the ball is hit his way. A football player must merely memorize plays—on offense—or recognize them—on defense. Basketball and ice hockey have only five and six participants, so passing and moving options are more limited than in soccer.

It's a game requiring all players to make split-second decisions. No one can tell you where to run. You can't step off the field and spend 15 seconds contemplating what to do next. You must decide where to move and what to do every second on the field.

## SOME DECISIONS

Let's consider some of the issues you'll face in a match. If you have the ball, you must analyze whether you or a teammate is in the better position to mount an effective attack. And if it is a teammate, which one?

**Attacking Decisions**—Should you pass, dribble or shoot? If you decide to go at goal, should you aim low or high, to the left, right or at the keeper? Which shooting technique should you select?

Goal-scoring is just one of the many ingredients that make soccer so much fun to play. (Stan Green)

When attacking, your team must make intelligent off-the-ball runs so some players are supporting the ball carrier, while others are creating space. Furthermore, a few players must think two and three passes ahead. If they don't and everyone supports the man with the ball, you'll crowd the play. It is likely that the defense will then regain possession.

**Defending Decisions**—When defending, you must decide whether to mark a man, guard space or provide support. Which man, space or supporting position is most in need of your attention?

## A WORD TO PLAYERS

Sounds complicated, doesn't it? It is because soccer is a "fluid" game demanding on-the-spot decisions. In fact, I could write another book just on soccer tactics.

Through playing experience, and watching top-level games, you'll start to "think like a soccer player." At that point you'll find that you do much less running. The ball will do a lot of the work for you. And when you do receive a pass, you'll have more time and space to use the ball constructively.

But now, as you develop your physical and mental skills, this doesn't happen. Your team probably bunches around the ball, playing what I call *banana soccer*. This can frustrate both team members and your coach.

The solution is to spread out. When attackers are positioned all over the field, the defense must cover them. The more spread apart a defense is, the easier it is for an attacker to play. This is one of the keys to offensive soccer.

**Everyone Makes Mistakes**—But you'll learn these lessons only by making mistakes. It's instinctive to want the ball and to move toward it. It takes a lot of discipline to move away from the play when appropriate.

At the youth level, the most important lesson to learn is to think for yourself. Don't worry if you occasionally pass when you should have shot or dribbled. That's natural. Believe me, at your age I made the same mistakes you're making today.

When I used to play in the park with my buddies, there was no coach to help point out our mistakes. Also, there was no one yelling out instructions!

## A WORD TO COACHES

Do not tell a player what to do as he's playing. Unless he learns to think for himself, he will never become capable of functioning on his own. If you wish to discuss a particular decision with a player later, that's OK. Do it constructively. For example, politely observe that it doesn't make sense to dribble or shoot when tightly marked and an open teammate is nearby.

The time to coach is before a game and at halftime, not while athletes are playing. (Dan Herbst)

Sooner or later, players have to stop relying on the coach for advice from the sidelines. Otherwise, they won't learn to recognize what teammates and defenders are doing and how to best exploit opportunities. In fact, in most countries coaches are prohibited from calling out instructions during a match.

**Coach's Role**—As a coach, you must make the game fun, teach players basic technique, and discuss the components of decision-making. Don't be concerned with team tactics. Those considerations aren't relevant until players are at least in high school.

A lot of coaches spend time worrying about player positioning. Don't. Let everyone play every position, and don't worry when a player runs out of position. They'll learn only through experience, and they'll *want* to learn only if that experience is fun.

Let all spectators know that suggestions from the stands aren't required or useful.

**How To Teach**—You can help players learn to think. The best method is to set up practice games in which decision-making is part of the process. For example, the small-sided games that I played as a kid—and sometimes as an adult—are ideal. I've presented many in this book.

It's difficult for a child to decide whether to pass, dribble or shoot when there are 21 others on the field. It's a lot easier to make the right decisions if there are only five or seven teammates and opponents.

This is a time when you can *occasionally* stop the action to point out decision-making and technical mistakes. It's a time when you can remind players of the basics, such as keeping heads up when in possession. It is also a great opportunity to improve certain weaknesses. For example, if players tend to bunch, put a condition that all goals must be headed in. Use your imagination.

## PLAYING YOUR BEST GAME

Learning strategy is only part of the mental picture. Another crucial aspect is knowing what you, as a player, do best and how to play the best part of your game.

For example, I'm a very good passer. I can recognize openings 30 to 40 yards away and deliver sharp passes. However, my defensive capabilities and finishing skills are only average, at best.

Therefore, when a teammate has the ball, I try to get open behind him. This allows me to see my teammates upfield *and* the ball at the same time. When I receive a back pass, I'm able to distribute the ball on the first touch, when appropriate. If I were ahead of the ball when it was passed to me, I'd have had to look backward to receive it. This would limit my effectiveness as a passer.

Of course, I don't do this every time. Sometimes I'll break forward, especially when we're countering quickly and directly toward the opponents' goal. When I do that, I'm thinking "shot," or at least using the threat of a shot to draw defenders toward me before passing.

The key is knowing that, in most cases, I'm most effective at starting attacks, not finishing them. For my club to get the most out of my services, I must play the best part of my game.

In contrast, Gerd Mueller didn't run very fast or dribble around defenders very well. He didn't play much in midfield. Instead, we exploited his deadly finishing skills when he was near the other team's penalty area. Gerd usually played facing our goal. We played balls into his feet, taking advantage of his power, shielding talents and striking abilities.

Essentially, Gerd and I excel at one important part of the game, but we also have the ability to do other things. I can score goals and Gerd could defend, too. We've developed all-around talents by a lot of practice in small-sided games.

## MORE ADVICE TO COACHES

Deciding what position to give different players is deceptively easy when they're young. To win games, put a good, aggressive athlete in goal. Put big, strong kids who can boot the ball far on defense. And have the fast players up front. Let defenders kick the ball upfield and let speedy forwards beat everyone to the ball.

That is a simple formula for winning games. But you won't develop good soccer players. Youngsters who rely on physical attributes instead of skill will eventually stagnate. They'll be stars at 10, starters at 13 and scrubs at 16. Often, it's the tiny 12-year-old who must use superior ball control merely to survive who eventually becomes the outstanding player.

Think of winning as a nice benefit of playing good soccer, not as the ultimate goal of youth soccer. If winning is so important that it becomes the *reason* for playing, you'll find that enjoyment and improvement disappear.

**Vary Positions**—I strongly recommend that coaches play all kids at all positions, including goalie. They'll not only develop all-around technical skills, but they'll also have more compassion for teammates when mistakes are made. That's the formula for better individual and team play.

## MORE ADVICE TO PLAYERS

By mid-teens, assuming you've played for a few years, you should have acquired good all-around skills. By then, you will know what you do best and how to use it during matches. If you're smart enough to know your strengths *and* your limitations, and are determined to out-hustle the opposition, you have the makings of an outstanding mental player.

Sometimes, the smarter athlete can defeat the more skilled player. Obviously, determination and intelligence can take you only so far, especially if your techniques are mediocre. But a lot of very good professional players have overcome limited physical talents because of superb mental conditioning.

**One Example**—Perhaps the best example is my teammate, roommate and best friend, Ken Fogarty. Kenny isn't very tall (5 feet 8 inches) or exceptionally powerful (160 pounds). To the best of my knowledge, he's scored only once outdoors during his entire

North American playing career, starting in 1979. His ball skills are average.

Furthermore, his speed is below average, and he can't jump particularly high. The only thing that Ken seems to do well is win. I'll never forget the time when we played the Kicks and Kenny crashed heads with star forward, Alan Willey. Willey had to be helped off the field. Ken was streaming blood.

Even so, Ken played on as if nothing had happened. His determination and courage inspired the rest of us to play even better that day. It was a typical Fogarty performance. He plays with a combination of concentration and determination that few athletes can match.

## DEVELOPING CONCENTRATION AND DETERMINATION

The right mental game begins long before the match starts. You must develop it in practice when you make the most of every moment. It's present before the game when you warm up and develop a mental picture of what you will do to help your team during the upcoming contest. And it is a positive approach you maintain even when things aren't going your way. A positive attitude allows you to regain your form.

Concentration isn't daydreaming about scoring five goals in an upcoming match. It is preparing yourself mentally to be sharp and accurate when you touch the ball. Picture yourself doing what you do best. Also, focus on what you need to improve.

A good pregame routine improves the odds that you'll perform your best. But it's no guarantee. There will be times when nothing seems to go right once the game begins. This is when you must summon all of your guts and determination, and redouble your concentration. Anyone can play well when things are going fine. The test of a champion is to do your best when things don't come easily.

## PREGAME PREPARATION

An important part of my game-day activities is eating a good meal. For a night game, I eat early in the afternoon. I recommend light, high-energy foods that won't sit heavily in your stomach come kickoff. This means carbohydrates such as vegetables, pasta and whole-grain foods.

You want to eat something that will leave you satisfied and provide nutrition, yet not be too filling. It should provide energy for the match.

Getting plenty of sleep before a match is important, too. Get to bed early the night before a match. You need rest and relaxation to play your best.

**Warmup Exercises**—It's critical to be physically prepared for a match. No matter how old you are, you should stretch and jog before the match to loosen up. This warmup loosens muscles and gets blood flowing, dramatically lowering the possibility of muscle strain.

**STRETCH!**
A good stretching session before practices and games helps improve flexibility and lessens the chance of muscle pulls and strains. (Jim Frank)

As you can see from the photos in this chapter, there are some fun warmups using the ball. In one exercise, you get loose by jumping on alternating feet while touching the ball with the underside of the other shoe. Try to perform this drill *without* looking at the ball. It's tough, but worth the effort.

Another good activity is soccer-ball situps. Pair up with a friend and lie on the ground with the bottoms of your shoes touching. Take the ball over your head and touch it to the ground. Then sit up and *hand it* to your partner.

Standing back-to-back, and using two hands on the ball, pass it around your sides or over your heads and through your legs.

**SITUPS**
Soccer-ball situps are fun. For maximum benefit, it's important that players hand the ball — not toss it — back-and-forth. (Jim Frank)

Strong abdominal muscles are important for a footballer. Situps and leg lifts are great tools for improving your midsection. A combination of the two is to lie on your back, holding the ankles of your partner standing behind you. With the ball held between your ankles, lift your legs together. Have your partner stand with his hands held in front of his chest. As your feet and ball rise, your partner pushes them downward. Try to stop the momentum of their fall before they touch the ground. Repeat the procedure for 30 seconds.

Before kicking a ball, do some slow jogging. When loose, start sprinting, then jog again. Backpedal a bit, and then sprint again. You can vary your running to simulate what you'll do in a game.

**LEG PASS**
Another great exercise is to pass the ball through your legs to your partner. He returns it by handing it back over your heads. (Jim Frank)

**Warmups with the Ball**—Now you're ready to warm up with the ball. Work on some passing, shooting and defending.

If you are a goalie, roll a ball to a partner who is five yards away. The partner takes light shots so you can get the feel of the ball. As the exercise continues, each player takes a few steps backward until the goalie is forced to start diving for shots.

Just before the end of the warmup, individual players should work on any special tasks they'll have to do in the game. For example, whoever makes corner kicks should strike a few.

After the last minute instructions from your coach, you're ready to go!

**For Coaches**—You can modify the warmup tips just described. Don't make warmups too strenuous or too easy.

**SIDE-TO-SIDE**
You can also hand the ball side-to-side. (Jim Frank)

**LEG LIFTS**
Abdominal leg lifts are an important training device for the physically mature player. (Jim Frank)

## OVERCOMING SLUMPS

Here's how: Go back to basics and play a simple game. If you are struggling, make the easy pass and be successful. Don't compound your troubles by trying to do too much. If you lose the ball, you'll lose more confidence.

Concentrate on the fundamentals. Play tight defense. Move into good attacking positions. And make an extra effort to know what you want to do with the ball *before* you receive it. This way you can "play your way back into the match." Only then will you have enough confidence to execute a difficult pass.

## PROPER ATTITUDE

Whether you are slumping or having a fine game, maintain a good attitude. Don't be cocky or a poor sport. Don't kick opponents or the turf. Don't take your frustrations out on the referee.

**Substitute or Not?**—Even though youth soccer has liberal substitution rules, I think an athlete who is struggling should *not* be removed from a game. The best way to overcome the problems is for the player to confront them. In life, as well as soccer, it's important to persevere. Don't encourage kids to quit by replacing them when they should be told that they can do the job.

**Don't Coast**—Whether you are sure of losing or winning, do not coast. Knowing the outcome of a game is not a license to fool around.

In fact, it's a great opportunity to improve your play. That's the time to try things you wouldn't ordinarily attempt in a close contest. For example, I might try a left-footed volley or make all of my passes with my left foot.

**Blaming**—Athletes should never blame others. If a referee makes a bad call, remember that you can't expect him to be as perfect as you are! If a teammate misses an easy chance, encourage him and tell him that he'll score the next time. And if your coach plays you in the "wrong" position, prove you're a first-rate player who can excel anywhere you're used.

**Excuses**—There will never be a shortage of excuses at your disposal. Excuses are for losers. Winners seek solutions. Always try your best and maintain the proper perspective.

## ABOUT TACTICS

You may have noticed that I've had little to say about team tactics. There's a good reason for that—this is a book on soccer basics. Until you have solid technical skills, strategy is meaningless. For most players younger than high-school age, playing all positions is best—with fun and skill development being the only important considerations.

**About Formations**—One of the most common questions I'm asked is what formation I recommend for youth teams. In my opinion, there is no secret formation formula. The team that wins is the one with the best skills and teamwork.

That's true at the highest levels of the game, too. Brazil won three World Cups in four tournaments because it had Péle, not because its tactics were any better than other teams. **Most Important Strategy**—What matters most at the youth level is that players enjoy the game and strive to develop skill, teamwork and sportsmanship.

Remember, soccer is a game without restriction on player movement. All 11 players are eligible to receive a pass anywhere on the field. That's why millions of North American youngsters play soccer.

Coaches must never forget this. Practice sessions should mirror games and require the same types of skills and decisions as matches. The games I've described and illustrated will do this.

Finally, if you *must* have a tactic or strategy, try the KISS System. That stands for *Keep-It-Simple Soccer*.

## A FINAL WORD

I hope you had fun and learned something from this book. But don't consider it the last word on soccer. There's plenty more to discover. Think of this book your first step toward becoming a knowledgeable soccer player. Attend clinics. Watch collegiate and professional games. Ask questions. But most of all, have fun.

At all levels of soccer, the most important thing is to have fun! (Jon Van Woerden)

# USSF Soccer Laws

## LAW I
### THE FIELD OF PLAY

**1) Dimensions** The field of play shall be rectangular, its length being not more than 130 yards nor less than 100 yards and its breadth not more than 100 yards nor less than 50 yards. (In International Matches the length shall not be more than 120 yards nor less than 110 yards and the breadth not more than 80 yards nor less than 70 yards.) The length shall in all cases exceed the breadth.

**2) Marking** The field of play shall be marked with distinctive lines, not more than 5 inches in width, not by a V-shaped rut, in accordance with the plan, the longer boundary lines being called the touchlines (sidelines) and the shorter the goallines. A flag on a post not less than 5 feet high and having a non-pointed top, shall be placed at each corner; a similar flag post may be placed opposite the halfway line on each side of the field of play, not less than 1 yard outside the touchline. A halfway line shall be marked out across the field of play. The center of the field of play shall be indicated by a suitable mark and a circle with a 10 yards radius shall be marked round it.

**3) The Penalty Area** At each end of the field of play two lines shall be drawn at right angles to the goalline, 18 yards from each goalpost. These shall extend into the field of play for a distance of 18 yards and shall be joined by a line drawn parallel with the goalline. Each of the spaces enclosed by these lines and the goalline shall be called a penalty area. A suitable mark shall be made within each penalty area, 12 yards from the mid point of the goalline, measured along an undrawn line at right angles thereto. These shall be the penalty-kick marks. From each penalty-kick mark an arc of a circle, having a radius of 10 yards, shall be drawn outside the penalty area.

**5) The Corner Area** From each corner-flag post a quarter circle, having a radius of 1 yard, shall be drawn inside the field of play.

**6) The Goals** The goals shall be placed on the center of each goalline and shall consist of two upright posts, equidistant from the corner flags and 8 yards apart (inside measurement), joined by a horizontal crossbar the lower edge of which shall be 8 feet from the ground. The width and depth of the goalposts and the width and depth of the crossbars shall not exceed 5 inches (12cm). The goalposts and the crossbars shall have the same width.

Nets may be attached to the posts, crossbars and ground behind the goals. They should be appropriately supported and be so placed as to allow the goalkeeper ample room.

## LAW II
### THE BALL

The ball shall be spherical; the outer casing shall be of leather or other approved materials. No material shall be used in its construction that might prove dangerous to the players.

The circumference of the ball shall not be more than 28 inches and not less than 27 inches. The weight of the ball at the start of the game shall not be more than 16 ounces nor less than 14 ounces The pressure shall be equal to 0.6 to 1.1 atmosphere at sea level. The ball shall not be changed during the game unless authorized by the Referee.

## LAW III
### NUMBER OF PLAYERS

**1)** A match shall be played by two teams, each consisting of not more than 11 players, one of whom shall be the goalkeeper.

**2)** Substitutes may be used in any match played under the rules of an official competition at FIFA, Confederation or National Association level, subject to the following conditions:

a) that the authority of the international association(s) or national association(s) concerned, has been obtained,

b) that, subject to the restriction contained in the following paragraph (c) the rules of a competition shall state how many, if any, substitutes may be used, and

c) that a team shall not be permitted to use more than two substitutes in any match.

---

**Editor's Note**—The Laws reproduced here are used with the permission of the United States Soccer Federation. For more information write USSF National Headquarters, 1750 E. Boulder St., Colorado Springs, CO 80909.

**3)** Substitutes may be used in any other match, provided that the two teams concerned reach agreement on a maximum number, not exceeding five, and that the terms of such agreement are intimated to the Referee, before the match. If the Referee is not informed, or if the teams fail to reach agreement, no more than two substitutes shall be permitted.

**4)** Any of the other players may change places with the goalkeeper, provided that the Referee is informed before the change is made, and provided also, that the change is made during a stoppage of the game.

**5)** When a goalkeeper or any other player is to be replaced by a substitute, the following conditions shall be observed:

a) the Referee shall be informed of the proposed substitution, before it is made,

b) the substitute shall not enter the field of play until the player he is replacing has left, and then only after having received a signal from the Referee,

c) he shall enter the field during a stoppage in the game, and at the halfway line.

d) A player who has been replaced shall not take any further part in the game.

e) A substitute shall be subject to the authority and jurisdiction of the Referee whether called upon to play or not.

**6) Punishment**

a) Play shall not be stopped for an infringement of paragraph 4. The players concerned shall be cautioned immediately the ball goes out of play.

b) If a substitute enters the field of play without the authority of the Referee, play shall be stopped. The substitute shall be cautioned and removed from the field or sent off according to the circumstances. The game shall be restarted by the Referee dropping the ball at the place where it was when the play was stopped, unless it was within the goal area at that time, in which case it shall be dropped on that part of the goal area line that runs parallel to the goalline, at the point nearest to where the ball was when play was stopped.

c) For any other infringement of this law, the player concerned shall be cautioned, and if the game is stopped by the Referee, to administer the caution, it shall be restarted by an indirect free kick, to be taken by a player of the opposing team, from the place where the ball was, when play was stopped. If the free kick is awarded to a team within its own goal area, it may be taken from any point within that half of the goal area in which the ball was when play was stopped.

# LAW IV
## PLAYERS' EQUIPMENT

**1)** A player shall not wear anything that is dangerous to another player.

**2)** Footwear (boots or shoes) must conform to the following standard:

a) Bars shall be made of leather or rubber and shall be transverse and flat, not less than half an inch in width and shall extend the total width of the sole and be rounded at the corners.

b) Studs that are independently mounted on the sole and are replaceable shall be made of leather, rubber, aluminum, plastic or similar material and shall be solid. With the exception of that part of the stud forming the base, which shall not protrude from the sole more than one quarter of an inch, studs shall be round in plan and not less than half an inch in diameter. Where studs are tapered, the minimum diameter of any section of the stud must not be less than half an inch. Where metal seating for the screw type is used, this seating must be embedded in the sole of the footwear and any attachment screw shall be part of the stud. Other than the metal seating for the screw type of stud, no metal plates even though covered with leather or rubber shall be worn, neither studs that are threaded to allow them to be screwed on to a base screw that is fixed by nails or otherwise to the soles of footwear, nor studs that, apart from the base, have any form of protruding edge rim or relief marking or ornament, should be allowed.

c) Studs that are molded as as integral part of the sole and are not replaceable shall be made of rubber, plastic, polyurethane or similar soft materials. Provided that there are no fewer than 10 studs on the sole, they shall have a minimum diameter of 3/8 inches (10mm). Additional supporting material to stabilize studs of soft materials, and ridges that shall not protrude more than 5mm. from the sole and molded to strengthen it, shall be permitted provided that they are in no way dangerous to other players. In all other respects they shall conform to the general requirements of this Law.

d) Combined bars and studs may be worn, provided the whole conforms to the general requirements of this Law. Neither bars nor studs on the soles shall project more than three-quarters of an inch. If nails are used they shall be driven in flush with the surface.

**3)** The goalkeeper shall wear colors that distinguish him from the other players and from the Referee.

**4) Punishment** For any infringement of this Law, the player at fault shall be sent off the field of play to adjust his equipment and he shall not return without first reporting to the Referee, who shall satisfy himself that the player's equipment is in order; the player shall only re-enter the game at a moment when the ball has ceased to be in play.

## LAW V
## REFEREES

A Referee shall be appointed to officiate in each game. His authority and the exercise of the powers granted to him by the Laws of the Game commence as soon as he enters the field of play.

His power of penalizing shall extend to offenses committed when play has been temporarily suspended, or when the ball is out of play. His decision on points of fact connected with the play shall be final, so far as the result of the game is concerned. He shall:

a) Enforce the Laws.

b) Refrain from penalizing in cases where he is satisfied that, by doing so, he would be giving an advantage to the offending team.

c) Keep a record of the game; act as timekeeper and allow the full or agreed time, adding thereto all time lost through accident or other cause.

d) Have discretionary power to stop the game for any infringement of the Laws and to suspend or terminate the game whenever, by reason of the elements, interference by spectators, or other cause, he deems such stoppage necessary. In such case he shall submit a detailed report to the competent authority, within the stipulated time, and in accordance with the provisions set up by the National Association under whose jurisdiction the match was played. Reports will be deemed to be made when received in the ordinary course of post.

e) From the time he enters the field of play, caution any player guilty of misconduct or ungentlemanly behavior and, if he persists, suspend him from further participation in the game. In such cases the Referee shall send the name of the offender to the competent authority, within the stipulated time, and in accordance with the provisions set up by the National Association under whose jurisdiction the match was played. Reports will be deemed to be made when received in the ordinary course of post.

f) Allow no person other than the players and linesmen to enter the field of play without his permission.

g) Stop the game if, in his opinion, a player has been seriously injured; have the player removed as soon as possible from the field of play, and immediately resume the game. If a player is slightly injured, the game shall not be stopped until the ball has ceased to be in play. A player who is able to go to the touch or goalline for attention of any kind, shall not be treated on the field of play.

h) Send off the field of play, any player who, in his opinion, is guilty of violent conduct, serious foul play, or the use of foul or abusive language.

i) Signal for recommencement of the game after all stoppages.

j) Decide that the ball provided for a match meets with the requirements of Law II.

## LAW VI
## LINESMEN

Two Linesmen shall be appointed, whose duty (subject to the decision of the Referee) shall be to indicate:

a) when the ball is out of play,

b) which side is entitled to a corner kick, goal kick or throw-in,

c) when a substitution is desired.

They shall also assist the referee to control the game in accordance with the Laws. In the event of undue interference or improper conduct by a Linesman, the Referee shall dispense with his services and arrange for a substitute to be appointed. (The matter shall be reported by the Referee to the competent authority.) The Linesmen should be equipped with flags by the Club on whose ground the match is played.

## LAW VII
## DURATION OF THE GAME

The duration of the game shall be two equal periods of 45 minutes, unless otherwise mutually agreed upon, subject to the following:

a) Allowance shall be made in either period for all time lost through accident or other cause, the amount of which shall be a matter for the discretion of the Referee;

b) Time shall be extended to permit a penalty kick being taken at or after the expiration of the normal period in either half.

At halftime the interval shall not exceed five minutes except by consent of the Referee.

## LAW VIII
## THE START OF PLAY

**1)** At the beginning of the game, choice of ends and the kickoff shall be decided by the toss of a coin. The team winning the toss shall have the option of choice of ends or the kickoff. The Referee having given a signal, the game shall be started by a player taking a place kick (i.e., a kick at the ball while it is stationary on the ground in the center of the field of play) into his opponents' half of the field of play. Every player shall be in his own half of the field and every player of the team opposing that of the kicker shall remain not less than 10 yards from the ball until it is kicked off; it shall not be deemed in play until it has traveled the distance of its own circumference. The kicker shall not play the ball a second time until it has been touched or played by another player.

**2)** After a goal has scored, the game shall be restarted in like manner by a player of the team losing the goal.

**3)** After halftime; when restarting after halftime, ends shall be changed and the opposite team to that of the player who started the game.

**4) Punishment** For any infringement of this Law, the kick off shall be retaken, except in the case of the kicker playing the ball again before it has been touched or played by another player; for this offense, an indirect free kick shall be taken by the player of the opposing team from the place where the infringement occurred, unless the offense is committed by a player in his opponents' goal area, in which case, the free kick shall be taken from a point anywhere within that half of the goal area in which the offense occurred.

A goal shall not be scored direct from a kickoff.

**5)** After any other temporary suspension; when restarting the game after a temporary suspension of play from any cause not mentioned elsewhere in these Laws, provided that immediately prior to the suspension the ball has not passed over the touchlines or goallines, the Referee shall drop the ball at the place where it was when play was suspended, unless it was within the goal area at that time, in which case it shall be dropped on that part of the goal area line that runs parallel to the goalline, at the point nearest to where the ball was when play was stopped. It shall be deemed in play when it has touched the ground; if, however, it goes over the touchlines or goallines after it has been dropped by the Referee, but before it is touched by a player, the Referee shall again drop it. A player shall not play the ball until it has touched the ground. If this section of the Laws is not complied with, the Referee shall again drop the ball.

## LAW IX
## BALL IN AND OUT OF PLAY

The ball is out of play:
a) When it has wholly crossed the goalline or touchline, whether on the ground or in the air.
b) If it rebounds off either the Referee or Linesmen, when they are in the field of play.
c) In the event of a supposed infringement of the Laws, until a decision is given.

## LAW X
## METHOD OF SCORING

Except as otherwise provided by these Laws, a goal is scored when the whole of the ball has passed over the goalline, between the goalposts and under the crossbar, provided it has not been thrown, carried or intentionally propelled by hand or arm, by a player of the attacking side, except in the case of a goalkeeper, who is within his own penalty area.

The team scoring the greater number of goals during a game shall be the winner; if no goals, or an equal number of goals are scored, the game shall be termed a "draw."

## LAW XI
## OFFSIDE

**1)** A player is in an offside position if he is nearer to his opponents' goalline than the ball, unless:
a) he is in his own half of the field of play, or
b) there are at least two of his opponents nearer their own goalline than he is.

**2)** A player shall only be declared offside and penalized for being in an offside position, if, at the moment the ball touches, or is played by, one of his team, he is, in the opinion of the Referee
a) interfering with play or with an opponent, or
b) seeking to gain an advantage by being in that position.

**3)** A player shall not be declared offside by the Referee
a) merely because of his being in an offside position, or
b) if he receives the ball, direct, from a goal kick, a corner kick, a throw in, or when it has been dropped by the Referee.

**4)** If a player is declared offside, the Referee shall award an indirect free kick, which shall be taken by a player of the opposing team from the place where the infringement occurred, unless the offense is committed by a player in his opponents' goal area, in which case, the free kick shall be taken from a point anywhere within that half of the goal area in which the offense occurred.

## LAW XII
## FOULS AND MISCONDUCT

A player who intentionally commits any of the following nine offenses:

a) Kicks or attempts to kick an opponent;

b) Trips an opponent, i.e., throwing or attempting to throw him by the use of the legs or by stooping in front of or behind him;

c) Jumps at at opponent;

d) Charges an opponent in a violent or dangerous manner;

e) Charges an opponent from behind unless the latter is obstructing;

f) Strikes or attempts to strike an opponent or spits at him;

g) Holds an opponent;

h) Pushes an opponent;

i) Handles the ball, i.e., carries, strikes or propels the ball with his hand or arm. (This does not apply to the goalkeeper within his own penalty area);

shall be penalized by the award of a direct free kick to be taken by the opposing team from the place where the offense occurred, unless the offense is committed by a player in his opponents' goal area, in which case, the free kick shall be taken from a point anywhere within that half of the goal area in which the offense occurred.

Should a player of the defending team intentionally commit one of the above nine offenses within the penalty area he shall be penalized by a penalty kick.

A penalty kick can be awarded irrespective of the position of the ball, if in play, at the time an offense within the penalty area is committed.

A player committing any of the five following offenses:

1) Playing in a manner considered by the Referee to be dangerous, e.g., attempting to kick the ball while held by the goalkeeper;

2) Charging fairly, i.e., with the shoulder, when the ball is not within playing distance of the players concerned and they are definitely not trying to play it;

3) When not playing the ball, intentionally obstructing an opponent, i.e., running between the opponent and the ball, or interposing the body so as to form an obstacle to an opponent;

4) Charging the goalkeeper except when he

a) is holding the ball;

b) is obstructing an opponent;

c) has passed outside his goal area.

5) When playing as a goalkeeper and within his own penalty area:

a) from the moment he takes control of the ball with his hands, he takes more than 4 steps in any direction while holding, bouncing or throwing the ball in the air and catching it again, without releasing it into play, or having released the ball into play before, during or after the 4 steps, he touches it again with his hands, before it has been touched or played by another player of the same team outside of the penalty area, or by a player of the opposite team either inside or outside of the penalty area.

b) indulges in tactics which, in the opinion of the Referee, are designed merely to hold up the game and thus waste time and so give an unfair advantage to his own team shall be penalized by the award of an indirect free kick to be taken by the opposing team from the place where the infringement occurred, unless the offense is committed by a player in his opponents' goal area, in which case, the free kick shall be taken from a point anywhere within that half of the goal area in which the offense occurred.

A player shall be cautioned if:

j) he enters or re-enters the field of play to join or rejoin his team after the game has commenced, or leaves the field of play during the progress of the game (except through accident) without, in either case, first having received a signal from the Referee showing him that he may do so. If the Referee stops the game to administer the caution, the game shall be restarted by an indirect free kick taken by a player of the opposing team from the place where the ball was when the Referee stopped the game. If the free kick is awarded to a team within its own goal area, it may be taken from any point within the half of the goal area in which the ball was when play was stopped. If, however, the offending player has committed a more serious offense he shall be penalized according to that section of the law he infringed;

k) he persistently infringes the Laws of the Game;

l) he shows by word or action, dissent from any decision given by the Referee;

m) he is guilty of ungentlemanly conduct.

For any of these last three offenses, in addition to the caution, an indirect free-kick shall also be awarded to the opposing team from the place where the offense occurred unless a more serious infringement of the Laws of the Game was committed. If the offense is committed by a player in his opponents' goal area, a free kick shall be taken from a point anywhere within that half of the goal area in which the offense occurred.

A player shall be sent off the field of play, if, in the opinion of the Referee, he

n) is guilty of violent conduct or serious foul play;

o) uses foul or abusive language;

p) persists in misconduct after having received a caution.

If play be stopped by reason of a player being ordered from the field for an offense without a separate breach of the Law having been committed, the game shall be resumed by an indirect free kick awarded to the opposing team from the place where the infringement occurred, unless the offense is committed by a player in his opponents' goal area, in which case, the free kick shall be taken from a point anywhere within that half of the goal area in which the offense occurred.

## LAW XIII
## FREE KICK

Free-kicks shall be classified under two headings: *Direct* (from which a goal can be scored direct against the offending side), and *Indirect* (from which a goal cannot be scored unless the ball has been played or touched by a player other than the kicker before passing through the goal).

When a player is taking a direct or an indirect free kick inside his own penalty area, all of the opposing players shall be at least 10 yards from the ball and shall remain outside the penalty area until the ball has been kicked out of the area. The ball shall be in play immediately it has traveled the distance of its own circumference and is beyond the penalty area. The goalkeeper shall not receive the ball into his hands, in order that he may thereafter kick it into play. If the ball is not kicked direct into play, beyond the penalty area, the kick shall be retaken.

When a player is taking a direct or an indirect free kick outside his own penalty area, all of the opposing players shall be at least 10 yards from the ball, until it is in play, unless they are standing on their own goalline, between the goalposts. The ball shall be in play when it has traveled the distance of its own circumference.

If a player of the opposing side encroaches into the penalty area, or within 10 yards of the ball, as the case may be, before a free kick is taken, the Referee shall delay the taking of the kick, until the Law is complied with.

The ball must be stationary when a free kick is taken, and the kicker shall not play the ball a second time, until it has been touched or played by another player.

Notwithstanding any other reference in these Laws to the point from which a free kick is to be taken:

1) Any free kick awarded to the defending team, within its own goal area, may be taken from any point within that half of the goal area in which the free kick has been awarded.

2) Any indirect free kick awarded to the attacking team within its opponent's goal area shall be taken from the part of the goal area line which runs parallel to the goalline, at the point nearest to where the offense was committed.

**Punishment** If the kicker, after taking the free-kick, plays the ball a second time before it has been touched or played by another player, an indirect free kick shall be taken by a player of the opposing team from the spot where the infringement occurred, unless the offense is committed by a player in his opponent's goal area, in which case, the free kick shall be taken from a point anywhere within that half of the goal area in which the offense occurred.

## LAW XIV
## PENALTY KICK

A penalty kick shall be taken from the penalty mark and, when it is being taken, all players with the exception of the player taking the kick, and the opposing goalkeeper, shall be within the field of play but outside the penalty area, and at least 10 yards from the penalty mark. The opposing goalkeeper must stand (without moving his feet) on his own goalline, between the goalposts, until the ball is kicked. The player taking the kick must kick the ball forward; he shall not play the ball a second time until it has been touched or played by another player. The ball shall be deemed in play directly it is kicked, i.e., when it has traveled the distance of its circumference, and a goal may be scored direct from such a penalty kick. If the ball touches the goalkeeper before passing between the posts, when a penalty kick is being taken at or after the expiration of halftime or fulltime, it does not nullify a goal. If necessary, time of play shall be extended at halftime or fulltime to allow a penalty kick to be taken.

**Punishment** For any infringement of this Law:

a) by the defending team, the kick shall be retaken if a goal has not resulted.

b) by the attacking team other than by the player taking the kick, if a goal is scored it shall be disallowed and the kick retaken.

c) by the player taking the penalty kick, committed after the ball is in play, a player of the opposing team shall take an indirect free kick from the spot where the infringement occurred.

If, in the case of paragraph (c), the offense is committed by the player in his opponents' goal area, the free kick shall be taken from a point anywhere within that half of the goal area in which the offense occurred.

## LAW XV
## THROW-IN

When the whole of the ball passes over a touchline, either on the ground or in the air, it shall be thrown in from the point where it crossed the line, in any direction, by a player of the team opposite to that of the player who last touched it. The thrower at the moment of delivering the ball must face the field of play and part of each foot shall be either on the touchline or on the ground outside the touchline. The thrower shall use both hands and shall deliver the ball from behind and over his head. The ball shall be in play immediately it enters the field of play, but the thrower shall not again play the ball until it has been touched or played by another player. A goal shall not be scored direct from a throw-in.

### Punishment

a) If the ball is improperly thrown in the throw-in shall be taken by a player of the opposing team.

b) If the thrower plays the ball a second time before it as been touched or played by another player, an indirect free kick shall be taken by a player of the opposing team from the place where the infringement occurred, unless the offense is committed by a player in his opponents' goal area, in which case, the free kick shall be taken from a point anywhere within that half of the goal area in which the offense occurred.

## LAW XVI
## GOAL KICK

When the whole of the ball passes over the goalline excluding that portion between the goalposts, either in the air or on the ground, having last been played by one of the attacking team, it shall be kicked direct into play beyond the penalty area from a point within that half of the goal area nearest to where it crossed the line, by a player of the defending team. A goalkeeper shall not receive the ball into his hands from a goal kick in order that he may thereafter kick it into play. If the ball is not kicked beyond the penalty area, i.e., direct into play, the kick shall be retaken. The kicker shall not play the ball a second time until it has touched—or been played by—another player. A goal shall not be scored direct from such a kick. Players of the team opposing that of the player taking the goal kick shall remain outside the penalty area until the ball has been kicked out of the penalty area.

**Punishment** If a player taking a goal kick plays the ball a second time after it has passed beyond the penalty area, but before it has touched or been played by another player, an indirect free kick shall be awarded to the opposing team, to be taken from the place where the infringement occurred, unless the offense is committed by a player in his opponents' goal area, in which case, the free kick shall be taken from a point anywhere within that half of the goal area in which the offense occurred.

## LAW XVII
## CORNER KICK

When the whole of the ball passes over the goalline, excluding that portion between the goalposts, either in the air or on the ground, having last been played by one of the defending team, a member of the attacking team shall take a corner kick, e.g., the whole of the ball shall be placed within the quarter circle at the nearest corner flagpost, which must not be moved, and it shall be kicked from that position. A goal may be scored direct from such a kick. Players of the team opposing that of the player taking the corner kick shall not approach within 10 yards of the ball until it is in play, i.e., it has traveled the distance of its own circumference, nor shall the kicker play the ball a second time until it has been touched or played by anther player.

### Punishment

a) If the player who takes the kick plays the ball a second time before it has been touched or played by another player, the Referee shall award an indirect free kick to the opposing team, to be taken from a point anywhere within that half of the goal area in which the offense occurred.

b) for any other infringement the kick shall be retaken.